3-

The gift of Sam

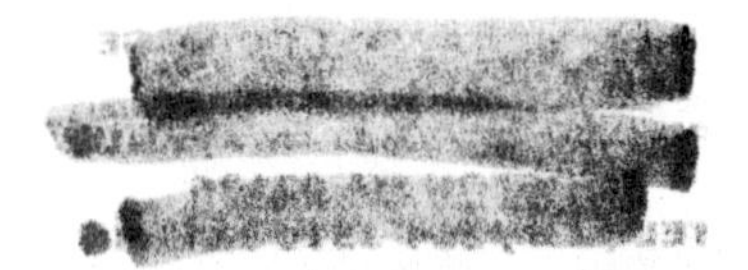

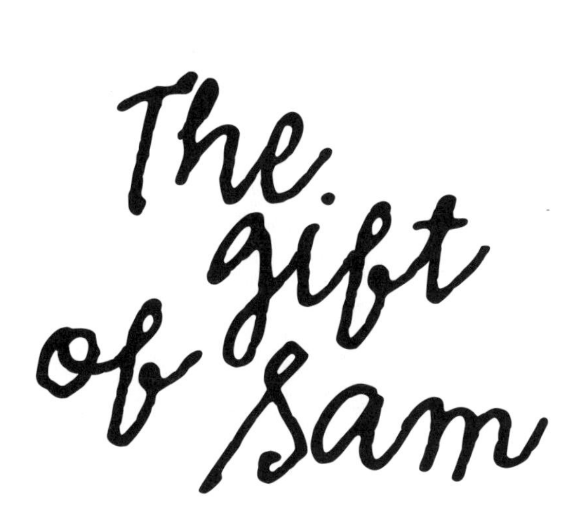

The Gift of Sam

a story of unspeakable grace

MICHELLE THOOFT

P.O. Box 181
Redwood Falls, MN 56283

First Printing 2002

ISBN 0-9723462-0-1

for Sam
May this book contain a lifetime
of love from me to you

Thank you

To my family for living through this, day in and day out, with me: Mom and Bob, you're the absolute best. Chris and Kelly and your fabulous husbands, my brothers: I love you more than tongue can tell: thanks for walking with me. Dad, Sue, Josh: for never leaving me and loving me in spite of myself. My dear "outlaw" family: the Thooft's. I'm glad I married into you guys. Louise, you are a true friend and inspiration.

My friends, Mary Urch and Meg Gemmell, my then-pastors, Bob Elam and Kevin at the free church, my advocate and friend, Pam; Beth my social worker and Anne my adoption worker, New Life Family Services in Rochester, MN, Mr. Hurley at WSU for passing me even when I failed the test.

Carson Haring, my dear friend : Samuel is named in part after you. Tim and Nancy Ramey, on their own road of suffering, for loving me through mine. May we emulate your love and gentleness. Lauralee Hansen, for all the long walks and knitting by the window. Deonte and Mary Jo, for the evenings by cookstove and gas lighting, tea and steak, quiet and northern lights. Kevin, for your friendship and being able to talk to coyotes: that is so cool.

The nurses at the hospital: you know who you are even if I've forgotten your names. You were truly are angels of mercy to this young agonizing patient.

To Sam's biological father: "What God is after is us—our laughter, our tears, our dreams, our fears, our heart of hearts."

To Don and Karen: I can't even think of enough to say of how much I love and appreciate you. Good thing we have eternity to talk.

Our pastor, Rev. Bob Henkelman and his lovely wife Pam: you are a joy to us. Pastor Brian and Elisha: what would we do without you? Everyone at the Redwood Falls Assembly of God: I have no room to name you all, but you all should be here. Everyone from Tuesday Night Bible Study: you are invaluable to us. You all are truly the Body to us; what a joyful community we live in. Cat and Jess, your lives encourage us to have faith. Pastor Orrel and Gini, for loving us when we were really unlovable.

Worldview Academy: Randy, Bill, and Jeff and their fabulous wives and families. Thanks for teaching me to see everything around me with a Biblical worldview. (See, Bill, grown-ups can be taught.)

Justin, for urging me to write. We are contemporaries! Andree Seu, for giving me your valuable time. May I someday paint like you. And for Lori Steinbach and your sometimes painful editing (here comes a colon just for you): I can't thank you enough. Jeff Stoddard, for your creative work and talent, and patience with my zillion emails! And finally, Janet Thooft. Without your work and belief in this project, I don't see how it would have come to be. Thank you again.

Kurt and Andrea: I can't put a value on your friendship. Cedar Campus, for the peaceful oasis.

My children, all five of them. Sam, may we meet again someday. Grace, Christopher in heaven, Ilsa, and Maddie: you are all forever precious to me.

And finally, to the two most important people in my world: my Father God, Jesus Christ His Son, and the Holy Spirit of God my comforter. Can I ever in an eternity express my love and thankfulness to You? Is it possible? And to my husband Phil. You are Jesus in person for me. The Father has taught me through you more than any other; your patience, love, humility and respect for me have healed a thousand wounds. You are what God "brought me to that I thought I could not reach." Thank you for being you and for loving me.

Being unable to defeat God through raw power, Satan's legions decide to wound God as deeply as possible by stealing the love of his beloved through seduction. And having "seduced them to his party," to ravish them body and soul; and having ravished them, to mock them even as they are hurled to the depths of hell...This is Satan's motivation and goal for every man, woman, and child into whom God ever breathed the breath of life. Like a roaring lion, he "hungers" for us.

John Eldredge

My window overlooked Lake Superior. I can still see it clearly. Directly below was a line of clay pots with hopeful pansy plants, then the deep, sloping lawn stretched about a hundred yards to the beach. This picture, framed in french window glass, was dotted with just enough birch and spruce to keep the lawn green with only patches of fragrant pine underneath. It was early summer, so my window was almost always open, and the cool breeze off the lake was like a reviving Spirit breath. When I wasn't working in the restaurant and lodge I was living in, the Lake Superior waves and the occasional lonesome call of a single, mateless loon were the only sounds I heard.

I spent many hours sitting in front of that window twelve years ago: reading, writing, listening, praying, crying, thinking. I grappled with God like Jacob wrestled the angel, dutifully following my thoughts through pain and suffering and separation and grieving and loss; all yet to come in my scenario. And yet, in that place, I learned to hear God. I began to understand more deeply what it meant that He loved me. I learned that I was not alone, like the mateless loon.

I was spending my summer at Naniboujou Lodge. I had spent previous summers there, earning money for college, and this summer was no different. But it was different inside of me. This summer I was alone and pregnant.

A month earlier during finals week, I had received the positive test result of my suspected pregnancy. This suspicion alone was shattering as I was a fairly active Christian on campus; a leader in various Christian fellowship groups. Worse, I had no boyfriend or fiancée. My pregnancy resulted from living a double life with alcohol and bar hopping and flirting, eventually ending in a one night stand with a man I didn't know.

One of the first things I did was to try and find a book written by someone who had survived this. Not a happily expecting mother and husband book, but something written by someone who was as terrified as I was, who was as alone as I was. Everyone said they were out there: didn't anyone write anything down? I found nothing. I left the store determined that I would write, and that someday, another woman would walk into a bookstore and leave knowing she wasn't alone.

My pen and notebook had become my constant companions. This was my first journal entry:

May, 1989
Winona, Minnesota

I'm 23 years old, a college senior, unmarried, and pregnant. I know from the start who I write these words to: you, a woman like me who finds yourself pregnant and alone. Everyone will be shocked, right? Nobody, especially you, ever thought you would end up pregnant. In my case, it was my first experience with sex, really sex and not just fooling around. It was an awkward, botched attempt, but apparently enough.

I was in the last month of my fifth year of college when I started feeling funny, and I got into the habit of taking a nap every day. I thought it was stress. Then I was late, and I'm never late.

After a week had passed, I went to our local free clinic with a friend and had a test done. It was negative. But the doctor couldn't explain my symptoms. She told me to come back in a week if nothing had changed. I returned and tested positive.

Since I had suspected, I believed I would be prepared for the worst. But when the doctor said, "well, your test read positive this time," I can only describe my feelings as hidden and hysterical; like a volcano that hadn't erupted yet.

Looking back now, I can tell you that although I sat there on that examination table fairly calmly, hysteria did indeed take over my mind. I reacted, I cried, I panicked. Darkness overwhelmed me. The doctor was sitting on a chair with her back against the door. I remember thinking that I couldn't get out. She asked me if it was a surprise, and I answered yes. Even though I had suspected, I hadn't really believed I could be pregnant. She asked me if I had thought about what I wanted to do. I answered, "I guess I'll keep it." She asked about the father. I told her I didn't know, but the fact was, I did know. I had met him at a frat party and hadn't seen him since.

"You do know that you have other options, don't you?" she leaned forward, seemingly in an attempt to comfort me. Her face was featureless to me.

"You mean abortion?" I asked. She nodded. "Where?"

"You can have one done in St. Paul."

"What do they do?" I asked hopefully. The temptation was huge: to have this quietly taken care of, not to have to face the humiliation. But something nagged at me that there was more to it.

"Vacuum suction" she said flatly. "The procedure is short." She leaned back against her chair.

Fear. Pain. Confusion. My head swam. It was hard to breathe. How could this be happening? There was no way out without pain. I had always found a way out! I could do two or three or four things at once! I had never hit a stone wall like this.

But something inside told me that I couldn't abort. Physically, yes, I could, but it wouldn't solve anything. I would kill a child. Why? So I could live with the pain of knowing I had taken a life - a helpless life- for the rest of my days? So I could face the possibility of death or mutilation myself? So I could be reminded of my foolishness and my selfishness forever? Because it would be selfish for me to kill him to cover up my own sin or to save myself humiliation or embarrassment, it would be selfish to never give anyone else the chance to love him. It would be selfish of me not to let him have his life. No one person would see, maybe. But God would see. He had known this baby before I had. He already knew his name, his life, his days. No, I would not abort this child.

I left the clinic that clear spring day sure I had made the right choice, but terrified of the road ahead. How could I be a mother?

Your evaluation of your soul, which is drawn from a world filled with people still terribly confused about the nature of their souls, is probably wrong.

John Eldredge

Still in shock, I walked three blocks to my sister's apartment. My mind seemed to shut out all other functions to try to cope with this bomb. What would the baby's father say? What would my father say? My parents were divorced and remarried: I had four of them to tell. I was the last person anyone would suspect of getting into this. Both my mom and my dad told me later that when they told their friends, they all guessed my other sisters before they guessed me. Everyone was shocked, because I was always the kid who didn't get into much trouble. In addition to being a steady "B" student, I never partied or even spent much time out except for youth group events. Once, due to a nasty letter written by me to my best friend in sixth grade, there was an uproar; but, until I was a senior in high school, that was about the extent of my mischief.

As a child of divorce, the center of my little-girl world was broken. Feelings of insecurity grew throughout my childhood into my teen years. Fear was with me wherever I went. Food met a need, and I was chubby. At school, I avoided people as much as possible, and then escaped home to eat and sit in front of the television. Everything seen was believed: in order to be loved by a man you had to be slim, beautiful, and athletic. This message was plastered all over the teen magazines I read and the television and movies I saw and the music I heard. My parents were trying to live with their own wounds and didn't know how to help me deal with these messages; they didn't know the struggles they needed to address in me. My mom was there for us as much as a single mother could be, working full time and teaching piano after school to make ends meet: she worked so hard and never complained. When we needed something, she stopped what she was doing and met our needs. She married a man who loved us like his own children and still does. My father was remarried, and although my sisters and I spent time with him and my step mom and later with my younger brother, we didn't really talk. I didn't hear the words, literally or figuratively, that I was beautiful or smart or fun.

So I began to believe the "message of the arrows" that John Eldredge and Brent Curtis speak of in their book, *The Sacred Romance.* The arrows told me that I was unwanted, unlovely, and that I didn't matter. They told me that my dad must have left because of me. My mom was awesome; how could he have left her? I must have been the unloveable one, the one who couldn't do things right, the one who was always in the way. The arrows told me that I was ugly, dirty, and a loser. Being beautiful or athletic enough to win him back wasn't possible, as hard as I tried. My journals of that time were filled with hopes that Dad would come back and that my parents would work things out.

Yet, all of this drove me to God. Somewhere in a deep place inside, I knew that He loved me, that He had time for me. He saw everything that I was, even parts of me that I didn't see, and He still liked me and accepted me, enjoyed me, even. He would sit and listen for however long I wanted to ramble on, about whatever I wanted to ramble about. I remember doing just that, lying in my bed at night, going on and on about my hopes and dreams and fears, and I don't remember falling asleep those nights. A friend of mine calls that "falling asleep in God's lap." He liked me, God did, and He liked to hear me ramble on. He had a plan for me, He had a spouse for me. How I knew this, I don't know. God himself must have told my broken, little-girl heart. Then He gave me the gift to believe it.

This was an example of the "Sacred Romance" in my life that

Eldredge speaks of. It was "something warm and alive and poignantly haunting" that called to me, "filling me with the knowledge of some Romance to be lived, an assurance of loves and lovers and adventures to be joined and mystery to be pursued." For however much I didn't see it then, I see it now: My Father knew, adored and treasured me, and He thought I was beautiful and fun to be with. He understood my thoughts. He understood why I did things. And He would never leave.

We attended a Methodist church that happened to be right across from my middle school. Many days, before classes began, I would go and sit in the chapel and talk to God. It wasn't praying; it was talking to a friend whose presence was deeply felt. He would hear fears of the coming school day, insecurities about how much or how little I was liked, anxiety over chubbiness or the abundance of freckles. Often I would leave flowers on the altar for Him. Then, after crying or talking myself out, I would leave a note for my youth pastor. John loved God and he loved teenagers; this was obvious. He pointed me to the Father many, many times, and he listened. Looking back, I see that some of the things I worried about then were silly, but John took them seriously. Through him, I heard the message of salvation: God created us to be in perfect fellowship with Him. He created us to be His friends. And because God wants us to choose to love Him, He gave us free will, meaning He laid out the rules and gave us the freedom to reject them. The first man and woman He created, after an unknown amount of years of close relationship with God in this beautiful, perfect garden, chose to sin: they chose to do what God had told them not to do. The fellowship was broken. But God still loved us and pursued us, even when we rejected Him. He sent His Son, Jesus the Christ, to die a painful death on a cross. Jesus took our sins on himself and paid for them with His death. He paid the penalty for us so we could again be in fellowship with God the Father. When we accept this gift and believe that Jesus is, He comes to live in us. When the Father looks at us, He sees all that He made us to be, unique and wonderful, and He sees His Son and His righteousness. We are complete. It's a mystery: Christ in us, the hope of glory. All I had to do was believe, and then God would walk with me. He had been pursuing me for years. I accepted this gift when I was sixteen. I tried to live as best I knew how, but I was a baby in my faith. This is probably why so many were astonished at my pregnancy seven years later.

My zeal remained strong until my senior year in high school. Faith had healed me of some of my fear, and I began to socialize. When John moved away, our youth group dissolved. I began to party with "the crowd." I was working in a restaurant with a friend who was ready to party anytime. She also had accepted Christ at a church camp, so we had a bond. But we were both immature and young, and sin crouched at our door, waiting to devour us. We loved God but didn't understand what it meant to live for Him. We didn't understand that our bodies were temples of the Holy Spirit. We got drunk a lot, spending time in bars across the river where it was legal for us. Alcohol brought a freedom from fear and restraint that I began to crave. There were many times that I put myself in compromising and precarious situations in our three-college town, as well as across the river in another big college town. There were always opportunities to get myself into lots of trouble. I am convinced that my first love, my God, was painfully watching me rebel, continually trying to remind me of His love for me. I believe it was because of Him that I was not date-raped or killed in any of the many near car accidents caused by my drunk driving. Thankfully, I was still cautious enough at this point not to be sleeping around. I was only flirting. How dangerous could that be?

Ephesians 6:12 says, "Our battle is not against flesh and blood," meaning that any person who may have said or done hurtful things in our lives is not our enemy. Our true enemy, Satan, is out to kill our hearts. Curtis and Eldredge state clearly in *The Sacred Romance* that the enemy's plans for all of us are the same: "to disconnect us from our heart and the heart of God toward us by any means possible...to kill the desires that would eventually lead us back to the One who loves us, using all the forms of shame, contempt, apathy, anesthesia, and perversion at his disposal." They call it "Satan's Grand Strategy." In some cases, the enemy uses small instances of painful words that sink deeply like arrows into the trusting mind and heart of a child. I lived my first thirty years defining myself by words that made me feel that no matter how hard I tried to do what was right, I inevitably did wrong. They were like tapes that were constantly re-wound and played in my head. Giving up thinking I could do anything well, I became apathetic and critical. There were times I didn't study for college exams at all, or even attend most of the classes, and I hadn't a care as to how I would score. It was simply too much to worry about. This filtered into all areas of my life. Why wait for marriage to have sex? It didn't matter to me anymore. Since I wasn't beautiful or athletic, the connection was clear in my mind: I wasn't worth the wait. Forgotten was the truth that Someone delighted in me for who I was. Forgotten was my first love, and I walked away.

We learn from the loudest messages around us, and the "message of the arrows" was just too strong and too believable. Bill Jack, a speaker with Worldview Academy, says "It takes work to think well." Understanding that I could choose my thoughts and control them didn't come until I was in my mid-thirties. That the Holy Spirit lived in me and could give me the power to walk in a way that pleased God was just too unfathomable. God wanted to shine His light of truth on all of my memories. He wanted me to see my past from His perspective: He was there, He was doing something, He wasn't silent. Today, the memories are still there, but the pain is gone. Jesus says that when we know the Truth, the Truth will set us free. (John 8:32) Satan had spent his time attempting to make God my enemy, and I believed his lies most of the time. Now I can be free knowing the truth that God was there with me all through my life. He had something to say during every instance; I just hadn't heard Him. I had misinterpreted my experiences. It has been said that 95% of the time, children misinterpret what they see and hear. Parents and other role models need to help them see the truth of what is around them and what they experience, or they are left to come to their own conclusions. Without someone to tell me that certain hurtful words weren't true, or certain looks weren't meant the way they were seen, I was left to my own judgements. When I wasn't validated, I was left to conclude that I wasn't valid. When my sisters were called beautiful and I wasn't, I was left to believe the opposite about me. When promises weren't kept, I was left to resolve that keeping a promise with me didn't matter. Do you see how it works? We come to many conclusions in our minds that are probably not true, all because we misinterpret what we see or hear and we don't have God's truth.

After high school graduation, I began studying at the university in my hometown. The absurd wavering between partying and flirting with various other disasters, and attending church and Inter Varsity Christian Fellowship continued. When a friend offered me a job in her pub, I knew I was living dangerously. Being a light for Christianity in a tavern doesn't generally work. It began fairly well, but ended working drunk and partying with a frat. My inconsistencies didn't escape me, yet they didn't bother me enough to stop me on my self-destructive path. It was still too much "fun." My Christian friends were great, but none confronted me on my double life. Maybe they didn't know. Maybe they were afraid of my reaction. Maybe they tried and weren't heard. Maybe God simply silenced them as He had his own plans for me. I don't know.

About this time, I remember hearing a sermon in church one Sunday morning that made me think about my life. Knowing that I wasn't living in a way that honored God, I prayed that He would do whatever it took for me to come back to Him. About the same time, and I can't remember if it was before the prayer or after, I had a dream. In my dream I was pregnant. The details escape me, but I was terrified and panicked. It was a dark and tremulous picture. When I woke, I felt elated. It was only a dream, it wasn't real. Thank God, thank God, I thought. Thank God it was only a dream.

As I walked to my sister Chris' apartment, I didn't feel the warm sun or the breeze on my face, drying my tears for the moment. Chris wasn't home; I waited. When she walked in that day, she took one look at me and said, "You're pregnant." I had told her of my suspicions a week earlier and she had thought I was overreacting. It was difficult to tell who was more miserable: the one having to face the crisis or the sister. It was all too heart-breaking; she wept for me.

This was torture: facing life every day with no control and all these unknowns and blackness before me. In those days, my friend Mary stayed with me. She literally stayed with me all day when she wasn't in class and slept over at my house at night. When I awoke in the middle of the night crying, she would be there. In the morning, when I woke to the darkness choking me and the flood of fear returning, she was there still, speaking words that said that I didn't have to fear, that God would take me through this. Survival seemed unreachable, and she reminded me that I would indeed survive. Looking ahead at the next nine months, of physically having a baby, of being a mother, paralyzed me. I had to finish college and I had plans for my life and a baby didn't fit. My mom had been a single parent; I had seen how difficult it was. I wanted my baby to have a mother and a father. How could I manage that? This baby's father probably didn't even remember my name. Mary listened to all this over and over, never seeming to run out of patience. She would just look at me with love and empathy. Then she would remind me of the truth. She was my angel. I couldn't fathom a friend so true.

Chris and I went for a walk that day, through our campus and town. We talked about motherhood, since I had decided abortion wasn't a choice for us (somehow I knew it wasn't just "me" anymore) and hadn't even thought of adoption. Chris knew that this baby was her niece or nephew, and she wanted me to have it and mother it. She came up with great scenarios: I could have this baby and we could get an apartment together. We'd find jobs with opposite schedules so we could take turns caring for him. Then, I'd meet someone who would want to marry me and father my baby, and everyone would have a happy ending. Perhaps they were a bit fairy-tale-ish, but they eased my load for awhile and gave me hope.

But I still had four parents to tell. Chris went with me to tell Dad. I had no idea how he'd react; this dreadful, empty, gut feeling told me that it would be sickeningly painful. But, he surprised me. After hearing me out, he simply hugged me and said, "Sometimes daughters make mistakes."

spring three

In my distress I called to the Lord;
I cried to my God for help.
From his temple he heard my voice;
My cry came before him, into his ears.
He reached down from on high and took
hold of me;
He drew me out of deep waters.
He brought me out into a spacious place;
He rescued me because he delighted in me.

Psalm 118: 6,16,19

Journal entry
May, 1989

As of now, five days later, I've told everyone. My parents, my sisters, my friends, my baby's father. I'm pretty lucky. They've all taken it really well, except my mom. She's having a rough time and she still doesn't talk to me much. It makes me angry; I don't know why she keeps everything inside.

Telling my mom was the most painful: she turned and walked away. I didn't understand. Now I see that when we are overwhelmed by something, we need space to digest. Sometimes we say things we don't mean when confronted and cornered. She was wise.

My mom saw what was ahead if I chose to parent this child, and she also had friends whose daughters had had children and lived at home. These grandparents had taken on huge parental responsibilities. My mom wasn't going to make that choice. "If you keep it, you don't live here," she had said. At the time I saw that as cruel and thoughtless. I had thought of living at home and parenting. Now I see that she was thinking for both of us. She would not enable me to be completely dependent on her. She knew my lazy tendencies, my immature thinking, my lack of knowledge of what it meant to make house payments. I was an adult, and I needed to take the consequences for my own actions. I have always thanked her for thinking of not only my best, but my baby's best. Years later, she told me how hard it was for her to give him up as well: he was her first grandchild. Yet, she stood firm. I am so glad.

It was then that the idea of adoption was planted in my mind. Over the next couple of days, I began to see adoption as a possibility. Not knowing where to turn, I called my pastor and he directed me to an organization called New Life Family Services. When I phoned, they connected me with a social worker named Beth. As soon as I heard her kind voice, the whole story tumbled out. She listened to all my questions, fears, and expectations.

I learned that New Life put their greatest care into the mothers and their babies who went to them for help. They offered post-abortion trauma counseling, help for moms who decided to parent their babies, and adoption services. They wanted to listen. In all my experience with New Life, no one ever tried to tell me what to do. They were simply there to help whether I chose to parent or place for adoption, and to advise me of the realities of abortion or caring for a child. If I chose adoption, I could choose parents myself. I could write them. Someday, I could meet them. Today, a birth mother and adoptive parents can decide on a plan that they are both comfortable with. A birth mother can meet her baby's parents before the baby is born, the parents can even be there for the birth. There have even been instances of a birth mother or father visiting the adoptive family after the adoption has taken place. As for finances, New Life had grants available, and I was eligible for medical assistance, which in the end paid all of my expenses.

Telling my baby's father was uneventful. Jack was a year younger than I in college and we had met at a frat party. We really didn't know anything about each other; I can't even tell you his major. He was "tall, dark, and handsome," but we didn't have a "night of passion." I've done a lot of things that I am not proud of, and hear me, reader, a one-night-stand is one of the most degrading. Alcohol dulled our natural inhibitions and common sense; in fact, most of the stupid things I've done have had alcohol involved. I had one experience with Jack, and then hadn't seen him again until I knocked on his dorm room door. I simply told him I was pregnant. He expressed concern for me, and he didn't offer any advice. He just hugged me and said he was sorry.

Journal entry
May 27, 1989

I'm finding that writing in this journal is my release. I know this will be for the good of other women. I'm doing someone some good. God is turning a bad thing into a good thing.

For the most part I feel fine, physically. I keep reminding myself that God is bigger than all of this and He will get me through it. Nine months to me is only a second to Him in the scope of forever.

But that doesn't mean I don't panic. That I don't get the hopeless, terrified feelings. A friend tried to talk me into keeping this baby today. She had a good argument; I'll be too attached, why let a stranger raise my child? She offered to let me live with her and her husband. She had me thinking. Will I always, every day, wonder about this child? Will I regret my decision? Honestly, I don't think so. I feel peaceful about adoption. This baby needs a mom and a dad who love God, and a secure home. New Life is so great, and I know that God is already preparing a couple just for me and my baby. I do have fleeting second thoughts, but I always come back to this.

Since things were tense with Mom, I had decided to spend my summer waitressing at Naniboujou Lodge, an eight-hour drive north of my home. I stayed in the staff quarters, and my room overlooked the lake. I didn't have much contact with New Life until the fall, when they helped me begin my "parent search."

The lake was healing. I moved my bed directly under my window so I could sleep in the moonlight and wake in the sunlight. I spent much of my free time walking trails and reading on the beach in the sun. I first discovered Anne of Green Gables at the Lodge and was entranced evening after evening, wrapped up in the story of the orphan who had found a beautiful home, family, and adventures. The atmosphere of the Lodge was peaceful, even on the busiest days. And I was certainly in an adventure of my own making.

God kept reminding me of Isaiah 41:10

> So do not fear, for I am with you;
> do not be dismayed, for I am your God.
> I will strengthen you and help you;
> I will uphold you with my righteous right hand.

I read this again and again. I had it on slips of paper in my waitressing notebook. It was a constant reminder that I wasn't alone.

summer one

Gently You come, softly You draw
And my heart burns to know You more
Can this be true?
Is this for real?
That You would love me, heal me, free me
Take me in?

This broken reed, this flickering flame
You have redeemed and freed from shame
Can this be true?
Is this for real?
That You would love me, heal me, free me
Take me in?

David Ruis

Journal entry
May 28, 1989

When I think about my baby, I think of a small, helpless little person who needs me. I picture him sleeping in my arms and the thought of giving him up makes me nauseous. But then, I remember that I would be caring for him 24 hours a day. Forever. By myself. I can't do that. I don't want to do that.

I want parents for him that will tell him about me and encourage him to find me. All he'll have to do is ask and his parents can give him all the letters I've written them over the years.

God, I need you. Thanks for being so wonderful, for taking care of me through all of this. Thanks for taking me back. Please continue to work on this little baby's father. Let Your will be done in all of this.

I can't ask for anything other than a strong, healthy baby who will grow up to love You. As he grows, please protect him from all the evil in this world; there is so much. Please do for him like You did for me: making Yourself real to me at an early age, taking care of me, loving me. Please, please let his parents be wonderful people. Open, honest, God-loving, rooted, strong people. And please, Lord, let this child want to find me someday.

Journal entry
June 5, 1989

When I arrived last week, Kevin took me out to my favorite place, Pierre's. We talked over pizza and salad...he is an understanding friend and encouraged me to think about the positive things that God is already doing through this. This little life is not a mistake! What my baby's father and I did was wrong, but God is forming this child. He's a miracle. He's about 3/4 of an inch long.

It's amazing what I didn't know. In that 3/4 of an inch, his little heart was already beating. His eyes were developed, his nervous system all laid out, his ears and nose were forming, his skeleton almost complete, and brain waves could have been recorded. He depended on me to keep him safe and warm. My six-week-old baby was not just a "mass of tissue;" he was a tiny, perfectly formed human being.

While at Naniboujou, I met a woman named Marli* and told her of my pregnancy. We talked for hours. I discovered that she had been pregnant also, and that our babies would have been about a year apart, if Marli would not have aborted her baby. She told me that she hadn't wanted to abort, that she was afraid, she was alone, she felt she couldn't tell anyone. If she had known someone like me, she thought she would have had the courage to go through with the pregnancy. She told me that her car had even broken down on the way to the clinic, and she had had to reschedule. Looking back, she had felt the calling and shouting of God to stop, wait, trust. But she had gone through with the abortion.

Marli said that the pain was excruciating. She said that the doctors and nurses were indifferent and unemotional. She felt like another number on their list. They didn't tell her about the pain. They didn't tell her that she would still feel pregnant, that her body would grieve the loss of her child. They didn't tell her that she would spend the next year buried in guilt and pain and loss. Marli wanted so desperately for the abortion to have failed; she had heard that sometimes that happened, and she was longing for her baby back. The grief was almost more than I could bear. She said to me, "I wonder what was *in me* that enabled me to do that?" I would say that the same thing that was in her was, and is, in all humanity: sin. We all have it, like a disease. When people tell me they don't believe that all mankind is marred by sin, I simply ask: Do you have to teach a child to disobey? To misbehave? No. We don't need to teach lying and stealing and killing. We are all born with these capacities. Rather, we need to teach self control, selflessness, honesty, humility, and integrity. What was in my friend that enabled her to abort her baby is the same thing that enabled me to consider aborting mine.

I actually felt lucky. My baby was alive. We had the same circumstances, but my baby was alive. What a gift I had! I had turned my back on God and indulged in the degradation of my body, and I had a living, beautiful child to show for it.

Since then, Marli has planted a weeping willow tree in her yard to remember her child. She is working through her grief, and is soon to be married. She has a beautiful, strong heart and a deep love for God, and I am convinced that He will continue to heal her.

*This is the story of several women: the names and circumstances have been changed to protect the privacy of individuals.

summer two

If the leaves had not been let go to fall and winter,
if the tree had not consented to be a skeleton for many months,
there would be no new life rising, no bud, no flower, no fruit,
no new generation.

Elisabeth Elliot

Journal entry
June 5, 1989

I'm feeling much better physically. Emotionally, I'm doing ok. Beneath all this bustle of activity in my day, I feel this deep loneliness kind of infiltrating. God, I know that You know what I mean. I can't imagine feeling betrayed by You, and that's how You felt: forsaken, forgotten. I know that I'm not. I'm so thankful.

One of my favorite writers and musicians, Rich Mullins, said, "It's okay to be lonely as long as you're free." It took a lot of pondering, but I think I understand.

Loneliness is part of being a person. It is part of living. I think that so often we run from any kind of pain or discomfort in our lives, and God uses these things to refine us. In order for gold to be refined, it has to pass through a fire. All the impurities are melted away in the heat, and what comes out is pure and brilliant. When we run from pain or loneliness, and try to fill the restlessness or emptiness with noise or activity or shopping or even drugs or sex or alcohol, we lose the beauty that could have been ours. I didn't know how to deal with my loneliness then and ran to others to meet my needs, especially after my baby was born and gone.

Since then, I have found a gem of a book called *Passion & Purity* by Elisabeth Elliot. She has gives practical steps to deal with our loneliness at any time in our lives. These are her words on how to deal with it:

Be still and know that He is God. When you are lonely, too much stillness is exactly the thing that seems to be laying waste to your soul. Use that stillness to quiet your heart before God. Get to know Him. If He is God, He is still in charge.

Remember that you are not alone. "The Lord himself goes before you and will be with you; he will never leave you nor forsake you. Do not be afraid; do not be discouraged." (Deuteronomy 31:8) Jesus promised his disciples, "And surely I am with you always, to the very end of the age." (Matthew 20:20) Never mind if you cannot feel His presence. He is there, never for one moment forgetting you.

Give thanks. In times of my greatest loneliness, I have been lifted up by the promise of 2 Corinthians 4:17-18: "For our light and momentary troubles are achieving for us an eternal glory that far outweighs them all. So we fix our eyes not on what is seen, but on what is unseen. For what is seen is temporary, but what is unseen is eternal." This is something to thank God for. This loneliness itself, which seems a weight, will be far outweighed by glory.

Refuse self-pity. Refuse it absolutely. It is a deadly thing with power to destroy you. Turn your thoughts to Christ who has already carried your griefs and sorrows.

Accept your loneliness. It is one stage, and only one stage on a journey that brings you to God. It will not always last.

Offer up your loneliness to God, as the little boy offered to Jesus his five loaves and two fishes. God can transform it for the good of others.

Do something for someone else. No matter who or where you are, there is something you can do, somebody who needs you. Pray that you may be an instrument of God's peace, that where there is loneliness you may bring joy.

Elisabeth goes on to say, "The important thing is to receive this moment's experience with both hands. Don't waste it. 'Wherever you are, be all there...live to the hilt every situation you believe to be the will of God.'"

If we were to stop and consider, what are our choices? When faced with loneliness or pain, what can we do? We can ignore it, surely. Then it would sift itself down into our gut and swill there like nausea, and we would walk around with this vague sense of unrest and illness. We can rebel and choose to believe that God doesn't love us. We can reject God and His plan and choose to go our own way. Or we can choose faith and trust that God knows what He's doing. We can accept and know that God loves us. He likes us. He is mostly glad when He looks at us. We are His "glorious ones, in whom is all His delight." (Psalm 16:3) He made us because He wanted to.

We have been trained to be like zombies that accept and believe whatever is presented. Did the six o'clock news say it? Then it must be true. Did *Mademoiselle* print an article on it? Then it must be right. Is our favorite "movie star" or "rock star" doing it? Then it must be good. Or even more close to home, are our friends doing it, or talking about it? Then it has to be the thing to do...or wear...or believe.

Understand that truth is always true. If truth changes from

one person to another, then it's not truth anymore. God can't be true for one person and not true for another: someone would be wrong. It can't be right for one person to steal from you and lie about it, because it wronged you. There is one way of truth in our universe, and God has laid it all out for us in His Word. There is right, and there is wrong: for everyone. Not all the messages we receive are true, and we need to sort them. We must embrace the good and make it part of us, and reject the destructive, deceiving thoughts and replace them with the truth. We need to know and see the truth about everything: ourselves, our world, and God. When we embrace the truth, our lives have meaning and purpose and beauty. That's how God made it to be. That is freedom.

We are created to live in freedom and truth. We yearn for beauty because we were created for a garden. In the garden, when God made man, He made us in "His image." We rebel against inconsistency and hypocrisy, because God is consistent and solid. We recoil at injustice because God is just. Deep in our beings we fight to save life because God is life. We spend our days searching for a soul mate because we were created for perfect fellowship with the Lover of our souls. We long for adventure and excitement because God is neither tame nor predictable. We look for simplicity and peace because God clothes the daisies.

Freedom is living and seeing everything around us from the perspective of God, who is Truth. Truth casts light on everything, and only then does everything begin to make sense. Loneliness is just part of our life here and we don't need to be afraid of it. We need to embrace it.

"It's okay to be lonely as long as you're free."

summer three

I consider that our present sufferings are not worth comparing with the glory that will be revealed in us.

the Apostle Paul, Romans 8:18

Journal entry
June 19, 1989

Sometimes when I sit and really think about it, this wave of darkness crashes down. All around me the birds are singing and the sky is deep blue and the sun is bright...it is one of those perfect North Shore days. It's times like this that I feel cheated: like I should be as carefree as the waves.

A worldview is the way a person sees God and the way a person sees man. Our worldview is like a pair of glasses we wear that help us to interpret everything around us, according to Randy Sims of Worldview Academy. Suffering has purpose in the Biblical worldview. All other views of God and man attempt to avoid or even disregard suffering, but God uses suffering for our good. The Bible says that we are to "suffer for Him" (Philippians 1:29), and that "if we suffer as a Christian, do not be ashamed, but praise God that you bear that name." (1 Peter 4:16) The apostles rejoiced "because they had been counted worthy of suffering disgrace for the Name," (Acts 5:41). God saw it fitting to make the "author of our salvation perfect through suffering," (Hebrews 2:10) and we are to "share in His sufferings in order that we may also share in His glory." (Romans 8:17)

What kind of God would allow, even want His people to suffer? Dorothy Sayer explains:

> Here Christianity has its enormous advantage over every other religion in the world. It is the only religion that gives value to evil and suffering. It affirms - not like Christian Science, that evil has no real existence, nor yet, like Buddhism, that good consists in a refusal to experience evil - but that perfection is attained through the active and positive effort to wrench a real good out of a real evil.

God allows suffering in our lives so that His glory might be displayed in us. Yes, my pregnancy was in part a consequence for my sin, but I could have easily not gotten pregnant and continued in my sin only to have it lead me down the road to even greater pain and loss. I believe my pregnancy was a gift. I believe that a merciful God intervened in my self-destructive path and instead of AIDS or another sexually transmitted disease, He gave me a child. We tend to wake up and choose another road when we hit a stone wall, and that is exactly what happened to me.

In the middle of suffering for my own sin, I was also suffering for Christ. As a Christian, I was called to a life that was set apart from the way most of the world lives, and I was displaying constant physical evidence of the opposite. There were those who wondered at my Christianity as I was getting larger around my middle with no ring on my finger. But I was not to be ashamed, for there was now "no condemnation for those who are in Christ." (Romans 8:1) It was a lot easier to say "I got myself into this, I don't deserve to have God get me out of it," rather than lay down my pride and accept God's love and forgiveness and live life with my head up. Really, all of us do get ourselves into our various scrapes, and none of us deserve to have God bail us out. That's what He does, because He loves, and we have to reject our pride and accept. I had to show up at church and Bible studies with obvious evidence that I hadn't led a perfect life. I could relate to women in the Bible like Bathsheba and Rahab. Both had led tainted lives, both were redeemed by a merciful God, and both were placed in the lineage of Christ. So much for Christians being "perfect." As an example, some have apologized for swearing in my presence. I wonder at this because it really is saying that they think I am somehow innocent or that they are tarnishing my ears with their words. The truth is so opposite: I understand my fallen nature. No one need apologize to me for their behavior; I am not perfect and I know I am not. As Christians, we are on the path to perfection, but "if we claim to be without sin, we deceive ourselves and the truth is not in us." (1 John 1:8)

J.F. Baldwin, in his book *The Deadliest Monster*, gives a clear definition of the "problem of suffering":

> Non-Christians love to use the 'problem of evil' to embarrass Christians. They often ask us why, if God is both holy and all powerful, bad things happen. But evil is really the world's problem. If the God of the Bible does not exist, what can the world say to the suffering individual? But if God exists, man may find profound comfort in the knowledge that He is in control and is bringing all of history together toward His appointed end. The horrible suffering of Christ on the cross brought about more good than if suffering had never been brought into existence by the rebellion of men and angels, thanks to the grace of God. Without this grace, what reason can any man find to endure suffering?

Douglas John Hall writes that, "God's problem is not that God is not able to do certain things. God's problem is that God loves. Love complicates the life of God as it complicates every life." God could have easily enabled me to avoid getting pregnant. He could have changed the circumstances so that I wouldn't have made the choice I did that night. But He loved me too much to manipulate my life or try to control me. God wants lovers, not puppets.

My great consolation is the knowledge that God used suffering to drive me to Him and bring about greater depth and joy to my life. He used suffering. In other words, He was in perfect control of it. It didn't have the upper hand on God. Granted, I'm the one who chose to do the thing that caused me pain, but God, who could have allowed death, gave me life instead. My suffering didn't have death at the end, it had a child at the end. It had purpose. Useless, forgotten suffering is worse than painful. It suggests that we have been abandoned to meaningless nothingness. This thought causes us great anguish because our souls were made to know God: He never intended for us to be alone. Therefore, when we don't know Him and we suffer, the despair is sharp.

My journal goes on to say:

> But then, I force myself to remember the night that all the northern lights lit up the sky and God said, "Look, Michelle. See what I do. I command the sky to bring beauty like this. I am bigger than you. I can handle your life.
>
> If I just calm my spirit for awhile from all the giddiness of daily life and look and see what God has done, if I take the time to ingest His promises, I see that He is in control.
>
> God, take my heart. You understand me, you know what I need. Please help me because I want to be entirely yours...

I really do. But I know myself. I remember how many times I've fallen backwards. I know how much I enjoy "sin" and the lifestyle it brings. Lord, I just have to trust that you'll bring wonderful things. I know, even though I don't always feel, that if I seek You, You will show me. Please help me never to stop seeking. I want to love You, Lord.

I am seeing that the more I get to know my God, the more boring sin seems to me. The less time I spend with Him, the more beauty I miss. To exchange life with Him for my old lifestyle is unthinkable: it would be like a dog returning to its own vomit.

Self-pity is the myth that we don't deserve what is happening to us, that somehow we are so good that evil hasn't a right to touch us. When or where did we get this thinking? We aren't "good." Romans 3:23 says, "...for all have sinned and fall short of the glory of God." And we are to expect trouble. Jesus says in John 16:33: "In this world you will have trouble. But take heart! I have overcome the world."

Indeed, and what a comfort. We will have trouble, so expect it; but when it comes, remember that He has overcome it.

Journal entry
June 20, 1989
Nine weeks

I have to remember that this baby is God's, not mine. Sure, he's coming from me, but God allowed him to happen, not me. He's forming him, He knows his little personality, He knows all the days of his life. He's a wanted child. He will touch a lot of lives. It took something like this to knock some sense back into me. I had all the right words for Christianity, but none of it was in my heart. It didn't come out in my actions.

Journal entry
August 29, 1989

Little baby, you are getting so big. Starting about a week ago, I can feel you all the time. It's getting harder to get out of bed, because my muscles are all stretched over you and they're not working as well. I'm finding I have to use my arms and legs more.

I hope you love me someday. I hope your parents are the kind of people who tell you every day how much I love you and want to be part of your life when you're ready. But I know that giving you to them is the right thing to do, for us. I am choosing to believe that God has the best parents in the world picked out for you. I want them to raise you like I wish I could, so we're probably a lot alike. They're just older and wiser and more settled than I am.

I think I freaked you out when I sneezed just now. You kind of rumbled, like I woke you up or something. You've been nudging me, too. It feels like your little feet are about an inch long. You're probably laughing at that now; if you're like your father at all you'll be big and tall.

You know, I never saw you as a mistake. Never. What your dad and I did was a mistake; giving part of ourselves away like that. Violating God's laws that are there to protect us. It only brought us pain. But you...you are the blessing that Jesus brought me even when I was walking away from Him. He brought you: a joy to me and a joy to your parents.

Don't worry, I don't expect you to be perfect. You may not even see things the way I do. I hope you're not angry with me. Because of you, I am back to everything that means something to me. One reason you came was to help your mom get her life together and grow up a little. Through having you, I see that with God all things are possible. Yes, I am giving part of myself to your parents when I give them you. But you are a gift I was never meant to keep. Be glad, baby. God has already used you more than you know.

So you see, you are special. In God's eyes, you were planned. I remember asking God one day, when I knew my life was headed down the wrong path, to do whatever He had to. I didn't want to come back to Him , but I wanted to *want* to. Do you know what I mean? He granted that prayer with you. You were not a mistake, and you will never be seen as one.

After all that God has done for me through you, I could never keep you and force you to live the kind of life we would have. Not that we wouldn't love each other, but it just wouldn't be the best. You deserve a daddy. You wouldn't have one with me. You would be stuck in day care all the time, being raised by people I don't know. Oh, baby, I can't do it. I want you to have a mommy and a daddy. Then, when you're ready, you can have me, too. I'll let you grow up in their love first. But I will miss you. I'll miss you so much.

autumn one

Because of the Lord's Great love
we are not consumed
for his compassions never fail
they are new every morning;
Great is your faithfulness.

Lamentations 3:22-23

At the end of August, 1989, I packed up and headed back to Winona. I didn't want to leave; the North Shore felt like my home, but I was looking forward to a weekend trip up with friends.

I started school, taking my last two literature classes. My professors and fellow students were heartening. I came to class one day and found a flower on my chair, from a friend who "just wanted to see me smile a little." Later, he told me that a former girlfriend had aborted their baby, and it was still painful for him. He was proud of me for allowing my child to live. I was so touched by the gesture.

During this time, I started searching for the "perfect parents." I filled out a form outlining what qualities I was looking for in parents for my baby. Then Beth and the adoption worker, Anne, matched up my requirements with those couples who seemed to fit best. Next, I received these "summaries" three at a time to look over. They all had code names: MT, AZ, PQ. The summary detailed things like parenting and education philosophies, type of home they lived in, their church and hobbies, each spouse's description of the other, and minors like nationality and hair color. I had this choice narrowed down to two, although they didn't seem to be exactly what I was looking for. Then Beth called me and said they had one more for me to look at: a couple who had just been returned to the pool because the girl who had chosen them had changed her mind at the last minute and decided to parent. This couple, called XL, had been chosen and disappointed three times in the course of seven months.

As written to me by Beth, "Because this couple is such a

prayer warrior couple, they always sacrificed their will for the girl and baby's best. The family always trusted God that those babies were closed doors. It showed maturity, guts, and faith to work through it without a 'poor me' attitude or resentment."

That hooked me. They were everything I was looking for. They were mature, open, honest, down to earth. They weren't afraid of me; that I would come back and take our baby away from them. They trusted that God had a plan for them, no matter what came.

I was looking for a couple who would take a girl or boy, perfect or imperfect. I didn't want my baby sitting in foster care, rejected because he didn't have all his fingers or toes. When you have your own baby, you don't know if it will be a boy or girl: you are joyful with what you get, and that is what I wanted in them. I wanted them to love my baby as much as I did, right now. And I wanted them to love me, because we would be a family. I hoped to be part of their lives someday.

I had a friend who was adopted, and when she started thinking of finding her birth mother, her adoptive family put her through all kinds of guilt. I didn't want my baby's parents to be the kind of people who would say, "aren't we good enough for you?" when he was ready to find me. We are all family in God's kingdom, anyway. I carried him, I bore him, they would raise him. They would be his parents, and I would always be his birth mother.

X & L are the best. They are everything I was looking for. They have a strong marriage, and they were still married after countless fertility tests and disappointed adoptions. "My parents" turned to God for their strength in the midst of circumstances that could tear apart a marriage, or at least make for a bitter one. They knew that God had a perfect plan, and they rested in that.

autumn two

I will cry for the desert
When He's bleeding
from His heart and soul
Die for the desert
And remove my hands from what I hold
Deeper in my heart I will hear His call
Deeper in my heart will I give it all
Deeper in my heart
I will cry

Twila Paris

Journal entry
September 15, 1989
5 1/2 months

Giving up my baby is starting to become real to me now. Not that I'm thinking of changing my mind. This baby is God's.

He is with me everywhere. He and I are always doing things together. Like my relationship with God, I can't see him but I know he's there. I only hope that his parents tell him about me. I don't want to be a closed case after we leave the hospital.

Then I think about how happy this couple will be. I only pray they remember me. I hope they can satisfy his little mind: I want him to understand why I'm doing this.

It was really important to me that the parents love me as well as my baby. I expressed that same hope over and over. I thought I had chosen the best parents I could; I had no second thoughts, but still the nagging insecurities reared up at times. I think this is what I meant when I wrote that "it was starting to become real to me." I had to keep going back to what I knew was true. This baby was a gift. This situation was being used to grow me into a deeper relationship with God, and therefore to grow me as a person. I would come out of this stronger than I went in. It would hurt. But God promised to walk with me and strengthen me and help me.

The adoption horror stories did scare me, and at times X & L seemed too good to be true. But isn't God too good to be true? Yet He is all He says He is. I think that if we could comprehend all at once the greatness of Him and His love for us, we would blow up. But one day, we will see Him face to face, and "we will be like Him, for we shall see Him as He is." (1 John 3:2) This is unfathomable.

I expressed my concerns to Beth. One way New Life helped me with all this was to give me an Advocate: a volunteer who wanted to meet with me usually once a week to just talk. Mine was Pam. She is a mother of seven and a pastor's wife. We met once a week at a little diner half way between our homes. She would send me notes during the week, lifting me up. She prayed. I talked and talked and had a million questions about family, marriage, the upcoming birth, parenting. She was rather shy and introverted, but she answered my exuberant questions as well as she could. She directed me to keep looking to God, who wouldn't lead me into something that would break my heart. She pointed me to the Father's heart, and his great love. She never tried to tell me what to do, she trusted that my decision in the end would be the best. I valued that. I never felt pushed, in any way. The decision to give him up was mine alone.

Before I knew it, the time had come for my long awaited weekend on the North Shore. It had been only five weeks since I left, but it seemed longer. School was going well, I had chosen my parents, and I was feeling good. Things with my mom were better. I think the time away helped her as well, she could deal with me and my growing pregnancy easier. She was also happy with my adoption decision, although she knew it would be difficult, for all of us. This would be the first grandchild.

My college and Inter Varsity friends Mary and Meg and I rented a tiny little cabin right on Lake Superior, about a mile from the Lodge. We had a wonderful time. We hiked, hung out at the Lodge, took pictures, shopped, and spent many hours just talking. It felt so good to breathe the pine scented air again and to sit and ponder Lake Superior. It is wide, deep, unfathomable, mysterious. The breezes off of it are restful, yet when a storm arises, it is mighty and dangerous. I have a deep respect for this lake. It is beautiful, and it is good, but it isn't safe.

Journal entry
September 23, 1989
Six months

Baby, I wonder if you can hear the waves crashing up our cobblestone beach. Or the steaming of the gas stove that's keeping my feet warm. Do you feel the same contentment that I do here? I'll be curious to know. I'll remember these things: where we spent our time, who with, what we said. It will be so strange to be just me again after you're born, after you leave. Even though it's just you and I here, your parents are at this moment in my mind! Since God knows them, and in that sense has joined us all together, I feel like I'm sharing you now. That you were never just "mine."

I hope you realize how much I love you. You are such a part of me. A lot of people say I'm doing such a loving thing, giving you up. Unselfish. But I've thought about it a lot and I don't think that's one hundred percent true. Either way, I'm being both selfish and unselfish. It's unselfish because some could say that I'm only thinking of you and not of my pain. To raise you I would sacrifice, and that would be unselfish. But keeping you could be seen as selfish because I couldn't bear to be without you. Giving you up because I want my own life could be seen as selfish. See what I mean?

It doesn't matter. I thought and talked and thought and cried and prayed until I felt comfortable with a decision. It was a decision made by me. I really am doing my best.

Someday, I would like to come here with you. I'd like to show you all the things I love and see if you love them too. Dark, starry skies, northern lights, Superior's waves, the smells of clean air and pine. Isn't it amazing to think that compared to the love of God, all that is just "stuff?" We will sit here, all of our families together, and catch up. I look forward to just watching you.

Well, baby, before you decide to wake up and start kick boxing me, I'm going to sleep. So I won't notice when you do. Do you know that you have the worst timing? First, you never kick in front of anyone else when I want you to, and second, you either kick during class, which is distracting, or when I am trying to fall asleep, which is obnoxious! I love you, Baby!

autumn three

We are frail, we are fearfully
    and wonderfully made.
Forged in the fires of human passion,
Choking on the fumes of selfish rage
And with these our hells
    and our heavens,
So few inches apart,
We must be awfully small
And not as strong as we
        think we are.

Rich Mullins

Journal entry
October 4, 1989

Dear Lord, my life is so good. It sounds so simple, but "thank you." I know there are people who love me. School is almost finished. Money is tight, but it's there. I'm giving a beautiful baby to a waiting couple. The reality of what I barely missed (AIDS, std's, abortion, rape) overwhelms me. I don't know how to thank You for such gifts. I love you, Jesus. Please make me like You. Teach me to love. Thank you for loving my baby. I need you, Lord; I would die without You.

I can't tell you, baby, how much you mean to me: you are such a part of me that the thought of losing you seems unbearable. But I know your little body and spirit need love and care. You won't recognize who is giving that love and care for the first six weeks or so. You won't miss me, you won't feel a loss. That is not your fault: none of this is your fault.

I want you to have a mom and a dad. With me you won't. You would grow up confused with a confused father, in and out of your life. He was cited for public nuisance the other night. I wish I could help him; for your sake I'll keep trying. I will do my best to forgive him and love him and be a real friend to him so I can tell you in all honesty when you ask me: we are friends. He's not a bad man, baby. He's just young, and has done some stupid things like me.

Me, who wants to be a full time mom for you. But how could I do that? We could live on welfare, but then where would we go? I could find a job and put you in daycare all day. Why? Why not give you a mom and dad?

I'm not the only one losing you. Your grandparents, your aunts: this is hard for them too. They don't really talk about it with me. Everyone waits for the first grandchild, and you're it.

I wonder what kind of person I must be to give you up. Will you hate me someday, or worse, not care at all? Will you understand? I pray you will. I feel this bond we have, and I pray it will stay rooted in your heart always.

Journal entry
October 18, 1989
Six 1/2 months

It feels so good to cry. I've been holding everything in lately. I feel like I've become this hardened mass of rock and flesh. Pam keeps telling me that my emotions are wild when pregnant. I can't help feeling that I'm abnormal, unfeeling, apathetic. She said that her toughest times were when she was pregnant. I believe her. I've shut everyone out except those closest to me, those I'm completely comfortable with. And even my family doesn't understand my faith. I wish they knew.

I don't like people touching me: you know, patting my

middle and asking "how's baby?" Meg did that the other day and I barked at her. I feel bad, now, of course. She was only wondering. I don't even like going to church because I am tired of being strong, answering people's questions. Do they really want to know how I'm doing? It's not that I don't believe my answers...all this happened for a reason, God has a plan, my baby is getting the best I can give...I believe these things. I know God loves me and has a perfect plan. But I feel so lousy.

Sometimes I am afraid, still. I'm such a wimp when it comes to pain, and having a baby is painful. Can I go through with this? I have to. I get so angry sometimes when I think of my baby's father and how he doesn't have to deal with any of this. He chose to walk away. Sometimes I think I hate him; I find myself wanting to see him hurt. I'm not going to tell him when our baby is born. Let him wonder.

I pray often for God to help me through. I just want to be normal again. I can't imagine being without my baby, I can't imagine ever being the same again. What have I done?

Journal entry
November 10, 1989

I just found a centipede in my bed and to me that is the grossest thing in the world. Well, maybe second, only to writing my Victorian Lit. paper. I'm lost.

When I marry and have children, at least I'll be able to warn my husband about how irritable I get. I've nearly abused our poor cat to death...he keeps getting into the garbage and climbing on counters. I almost caught myself picking him up by the neck today - good Lord, am I that violent? Pam says it's normal. I hope the humane society doesn't find out how normal I am.

Here you see some of my emotional ups and downs: I didn't need to feel so distressed about them. Hormones really do affect our thinking sometimes. And yet, the feelings I was experiencing were so normal; I was in a crisis situation. I mean, who thinks of these things in a normal, day to day existence? I had choices to make and uphold that would determine the outcome of someone else's life. That is a sobering responsibility for anyone, even in a happily wed, two parent family. I know now that I can choose my thoughts: I can "take every thought captive and make it obedient to Christ," (2 Cor. 10:5) but that took time to learn and practice. Even then, hormones and huge life decisions sometimes make things difficult.

The truth is, we are in a war, and the battlefield is in our minds. Sometimes it is in the physical, but for the most part, what we allow in our minds affects the physical. We read stories of Christians being tortured for their faith, and yet they have peace, because they wage the battle in their minds well. That means that they turn to God and His Word for their strength. They know they are loved. They know that the road is worth the destination. They know Truth.

Our thoughts are powerful, as Proverbs 23:7 says, "For as he thinks in his heart, so is he..." In Romans, Paul says that "those who live according to the sinful nature have their minds set on what that nature desires; but those who live in accordance with the Spirit have their minds set on what the Spirit desires." (8:5) We, with the help of the Holy Spirit, need to train our minds to think the truth. We can't give up on this, and it may take a long while, but God never gives up on us. Joyce Meyer, in her straightforward book, *Battlefield of the Mind*, tells us that "positive minds produce positive lives, and negative minds produce negative lives." We are what we think. She says,

> "I know that it is the power of the Holy Spirit working through the Word of God that brings victory into our lives. But a large part of the work that needs to be done is for us to line up our thinking with God and His Word. If we refuse to do this or choose to think it is unimportant, we will never experience victory."

Would I have been able to make the decisions I made if I had not turned to God for His strength, for His truth in His Word? I don't know. I cannot fathom having survived without Him; He was, and is, my constant companion. And I can honestly tell you, I have been thankful a million times over that I did things the way I did. Every time I get a letter from my baby's parents, with all the glowing reports and pictures, I am blessed. I am thankful I carried him to term and valued his life even when I couldn't see it. The key is to remember the difference between feelings and truth. The truth was, I was single and had no idea if I'd ever marry. I had no job, much less a career. I could've gotten a job fairly easily, but I could not be in two places at once. My baby would have to be put in day care. My sister had inspiring notions of living together and working opposite shifts so we could care for him, but what would happen when he was up in the middle of the night? The sister who would be up with him would also be the one who had to work in the morning. What happened when my sister decided to get married, or was offered a job in another city, or simply got tired of parenting a child that she couldn't really parent? I would have made my choice based on my circumstances, and my circumstances would have changed. The truth was, God brought Xylophone & Lollipop to me, and they had wanted children for years and years. God was answering their prayers through me. They had a strong marriage, a home, a family. Lollipop was prepared to stay home and mother our baby. She could be up all night and not have to be at work at 7 am.

Most importantly, I felt strongly that a child needed two parents. At that time in my life I was painfully aware that I would only be one parent, and I would have to be gone much of the time earning a living for us. My baby would miss out on the same things I missed out on. He would grow up wondering what it would be like to have two parents who loved each other and were committed to each other despite life's black arrows. They would be committed to growing emotionally and spiritually, so that they wouldn't grow apart. They would be a picture of Christ and his Church, here on earth. Even in a one parent family where the other parent dies, the children still have the memories and the truth that they are loved by the missing parent. My mother didn't get married thinking that someday she would get a divorce and parent alone. If I decided to keep my baby, I would be choosing single parenthood, when I had a better choice waiting. Furthermore, I had no idea what to expect of this baby's father. Would he be in our child's life? Out? Wavering? I believed that God had someone for me, and I could risk my own happiness on that; plan my own life for that. I could not risk his. I would not risk his.

I am convinced that something deep within all of us longs for a family. Little girls need their fathers. Little boys need their fathers. And mothers are indispensable. It was up to me to look at the truth squarely and honestly and make the best choice for him. Together with Xylophone & Lollipop, I could build a family. I heard many years later that another birthmother said, "I am not giving my child to them, I am giving them to him."

Here is the truth: Life is sacred because God is life. King David wrote this:

"For you created my inmost being; you knit me together

in my mother's womb. I praise you because I am fearfully and wonderfully made; your works are wonderful, I know that full well. My frame was not hidden from you when I was made in the secret place. When I was woven together in the depths of the earth, your eyes saw my unformed body. All the days ordained for me were written in your book before one of them came to be." (Psalm 139:13)

First, this child deserved life. Second, because I gave him life, I also had to choose the best life for him. That meant I had to look at everything, as it was, and with much prayer, decide. Regardless of emotions or hormones or the influences of people, the responsibility was mine.

Journal entry
November 7, 1989

Re-reading this journal has a sort of healing effect on me. In some ways it's funny how confused I have been... never about the facts, just about my feelings. It's like I always know the bottom line: giving you, Baby, to your parents is the right thing for everyone. But my emotions are constantly in swing! I'm grateful that the solid foundation will always be there and will always be true.

autumn four

Oh, Lord Almighty, if you will only look upon your servant's misery and remember me, and not forget your servant but give her a son, then I will give him to the Lord for all the days of his life.

1 Samuel 1:11

From early on in my pregnancy, I believed my baby was a boy. I don't know why, it was just that I couldn't imagine he was a girl. I had a name chosen: Samuel Carson. Carson after a dear friend, and Samuel, I don't know. It just came to me: it just felt right.

Journal entry
October 23, 1989

I realize now what the Lord is telling me.

I am like Hannah. In some ways, I asked for this child. I knew my life was going wrong, and I prayed that God would do what He had to to make it right. So He gave me a baby to carry for nine months, to mother for a few days, and to give back to Him to care for his entire life. I may never see this child again. I may never have another. Hannah prayed for a son, and God remembered her. Then she gave him up. She trusted God with her son: Samuel.

I decided to name my baby Samuel before I knew this

story. This is a huge confirmation that I am doing the right thing! Lord God, please continue to teach me to trust!

This revelation hit me like a flood. I had a vague recollection in my mind about the Biblical story of Hannah but I couldn't remember the name of her child. The story kept coming up in my thoughts, until finally I looked it up, in the parking lot of the clinic after one of my prenatal visits. Then, the doors of my mind were flung open and all of a sudden it made sense. Hannah named her son Samuel. My son's name would be Samuel. I had chosen that name months ago. She gave her son to God. I would be giving my son to God to care for. The parallels between her story and mine astounded me. It was so beautiful; that I would choose a name seemingly for no reason, and then months later God would show me the meaning of the name and it fit perfectly. God, the creator of the universe, had been thinking of me. He had my baby in His mind. With all the ravages of the world-famine, plague, murder, strife, hatred-He had time to think of me. A connection, or "confirmation" like that gave me confidence to move forward. It was like thinking I might be lost in the woods and all of a sudden finding that I was on the right trail after all.

autumn five

Piglet sidled up to Pooh from behind.
"Pooh," he whispered.
"Yes, Piglet?"
"Nothing," said Piglet, taking Pooh's paw,
"I just wanted to be sure of you."

A.A. Milne

It was time to begin writing "my parents." It was so exciting that I could put personalities to code letters, that I could actually get to know them before our baby was born. Today, things are much more open, in fact, they are as open as a birth mother and adoptive parents want them to be. My sister and brother in law have even taken the birth mother of their child on vacations with them. It's so much about family, and about giving a child the best you can, rather than holding on. Maybe I have said this before, but I have never regretted giving Sam a family. Here are our letters.

Letter to Adoptive Parents
December 21, 1989
Dear "XL"

I am writing this before our baby is born. I realize that this may be a bit frightening for you, thinking that you may get let down. But I can honestly tell you that I know this is God's decision for us. By communicating with you now, I am being assured that this precious child doing somersaults inside me right now is going into loving, capable hands. Being that God led me specifically to you and seemingly vice versa, I should have no need for reassurance. Just human, I guess, huh? I've read and heard the horror stories and I let them get to me probably just like everyone else. I don't believe I've ever been this concerned about someone else's welfare. This baby has taught me a lot. I have never had to make a sacrifice or choose whether to let someone live or die. I praise God that He helped me to make the right choice.

There are many thoughts that have held me to my decision. One was knowing, above all the confusion and pain I have sometimes felt, that this is God's plan for us. Another was imagining the joy I would be giving to you. How does that feel? What do you want to know about me? I want to share everything: I wish I could sit down with you and tell you the whole story from the beginning. I wish you could be there when our baby is born; I wish I could give him to you myself.

It's hard to imagine my baby growing up without me; knowing two other people as mom and dad. But I know it's for the best. According to Anne and Beth, I've been given a "one in a million couple" and I can't tell you how good that makes me feel.

There are so many things I want to say and I feel like part of them have come out in a jumbled mess in this letter. I'll stop here and wait to hear from you. Thank you for being the people that you are. Take care.

your birthmom

January 3, 1990

Dear Birthmom,

Thanks so much for your wonderful letter! For the sake of our writing, we'll refer to husband as "X" and wife as "L." Wow, sounds a little impersonal! One of X's first comments while reading your letter was "she sounds a lot like you!" We agree that God has been and is leading us together. Your "need for assurance" is wonderful. God has given us each a heart and mind to use to His glory. When we have questions, the Lord wants to know them and desires us to seek

Him and His strength. Your heart and relationship with the Lord is encouraging to us. We are grateful that you are desiring to seek the Lord's direction. While the world eagerly pushes the "easy way out" of such a situation, it takes courage to face the issue and make responsible decisions. We thank God for you and your love for Him.

We have waited for the day when a little person will be in our arms. The joy you will be giving us is beyond words; more than we can ask or think! One of our highest desires in life is to raise a little person, in a home filled with God's love, having that little heart and mind grow knowing that they are a wonderful person and thoroughly loved!

We want to be sensitive to a little person growing up knowing they're adopted and be able to fill in as much of the unknown part of their life as possible. You are and always will be important to us and "our" child.

What do we want to know about you? Where do we begin? We look at your letter and see the handwriting and composition of someone who's neat, organized, sensitive, loving, caring, creative! Sounds like we're analyzing your handwriting! It's strange when it's all we've got.

We're interested in who you are; what kind of environment did you grow up in, what things helped shape the person you are, what kind of person do you see yourself as? Anne has briefly shared some of your interests. We'd love to hear more! Who you are is going to be so much a part of our little person.

We both grew up in Christian homes where God and His love were the highest priority. We are from the same evangelical denominational background and met in early college days. I thank God often for our upbringing. Our families have similar lifestyles and goals. What we came from is a lot of who we are. Both families are loving and peace-centered. We make most all decisions together. X and I don't fight. We have differences of opinion, but we talk them out and they're done with. Neither of us grew up in homes where people "yelled" at each other. I am eternally grateful for his love and respect for me. I have never once doubted his love, of which I continually thank the Lord. He is a dear, dear man.

As for his relationship with children, they love him! Most of our friends call us second parents to their children. Some dear friends have three boys who think X is the strongest man in the world: the kids love to ride on his feet. He has a wonderful way with children.

'I'd love to add a bit about my father. I recently read an article that said "We learn best in an environment that gives us total permission to make mistakes." That is who my father is. As we grew and made mistakes, his gentleness in letting us each see ourselves where we had gone wrong (rather than preach to us about it) has been one of the things that has made me who I am. He is one of the two most loving, generous, caring, wonderful people in the world.

X writing now. I believe L will make a great mom. She has a special ability to communicate with children and make them feel loved and worthwhile. She gives children great personal attention and draws out the best in them. Her spontaneity and energy is a real motivator with children. I believe that our child will have a very good experience with L. I just had to say this!

Thanks for your letter. We are praying for you as your days come close to delivery. We are looking forward to hearing from you soon!

Love,
X & L

January 8, 1990
Dear X & L

It's hard for me to believe you're real people, having to refer to you as X and L! What if I call you Xylophone and Lollipop? If that's ok with you, it sounds more personal. I am so blessed and so loved, but my life has been quite different than yours. You guys sound a lot like my best friend and lamaze partner. I used to get jealous of her home where nobody fought! But God has shown me that He uses people from all types of backgrounds. I wouldn't trade a thing: my wonderful family, my parents and stepparents, my mistakes, or this child. I have learned valuable lessons.

I don't believe there has ever been a child more loved than this one. His little life has touched so many friends, acquaintances, family: so many people have come to me with stories. Women who have aborted have shared their grief with me and their joy over my decision, men who have had children aborted, teens who are confused about whether to say "yes" or "no," teachers who have asked me to speak to their classes about adoption, pregnancy, sex, abortion...! It's incredible, the doors to ministry that God has opened all because of this one child. And I have gained a respect for myself. For one of the first times in my life, I didn't take the easy way out. All because of Jesus, who loved me enough to discipline me in the form of a child.

I can't tell you how it comforts me to know how much you love this baby. I am not giving him to you because I don't love or want him. Please, please, when the time comes, tell him that. Tell him how much I would've loved to be his mommy, how I would've taught him to love and respect people and God, how I would have always tried to be open and honest with him. Tell him that I gave him over to you because you are a family. You are ready for him. God chose you for this. I was chosen to carry him and love him for nine months, after that, he was sent to you.

They say babies can hear inside their mothers, so I talk to him and we listen to a lot of music. Since I was a small child, I have responded to music. I can't tell you what this means. You know that bible verse that says the Spirit prays for us in groans that words cannot express? That is music, for me.

You told me about your father. He sounds wonderful. I am so glad our child will hear loving words from a father. My dad wasn't in our home, and I would never wish that on any child. My mom gave piano lessons after school to make ends meet while we were growing up. Looking back, I can't imagine how she did it! She sacrificed so much for us. It took me a long time to forgive my dad and realize that there are two sides to every coin.

I loved what you said about room for mistakes. I wouldn't be who I am today if it wasn't for the mistakes of myself and others; but most importantly, if it weren't for the love of a God who transforms mistakes. I want you to know: I am not the Christian I should be. I never have been. I have days of doubt, fear, and anger. "There are two of me: one does the right thing, one cannot see." Amy Grant sang that.

Well, the way things look, you will have our child within a month. I think he will be born any day. I have already started dilating and I've been experiencing false labor. I'm not looking forward to saying goodbye, but I am looking forward to starting my life. I finished up my B.A. in English and I have job hunting to do. We'll see where God leads me. Beth knows I want the hearing to be quick. She's doing all she can to speed up the legal process. I don't think I'll feel secure until this baby is with you and out of the shuffle. I want him to bond with you as soon as possible. I hope and pray that his being taken from me and then taken from foster parents won't affect him. I have been sewing for him; I made him a baby quilt and a sleeper to match my nightgown.

I fully agree with any course you take in telling him about me. I don't want to do anything that would confuse or hurt him. But if there is any way I could contribute or watch him grow through you, I would be forever grateful. One of my biggest fears is that he would be lost to me the minute I left the hospital. Judging from you letter, that is unlikely. I am so thankful for your love and openness.

Why did I choose you? I looked over many summaries, and there was always something I didn't like. I liked everything about you. Actually, I patterned my requests after a family that is very dear to me. They are strong, rooted, fun-loving, uncompromising, yet entirely human and not at all "religious." The husband of this family treats me the way he treats his own daughter. I feel such a part of their family. His wife has been incredibly supportive, sending gifts and cards out of the blue. He is adventurous and outgoing. She is practical and generous and gentle. And they have such a fun sense of humor. I love the comfort and joy of this family. You sound a lot like them. It sounds like you would raise our boy like I would, if I could.

I would love to keep writing and writing, but I'll close with what I know of the birth father.

We met at a frat party. He is a basketball player and a business major. He has a beautiful singing voice. It's hard not to be furious at his attitude, and he's had a few run-ins with my hotheaded sisters. Now, we talk. He's trying to be more open and honest with me. His family just doesn't want to talk about it. I believe he cares, he's just one of those people who doesn't know how to show it. We are friends, and I'll be glad to tell our baby that someday. I've tried to encourage him to write you; maybe he will.

I look forward to hearing from you again. You're in my thoughts and prayers.

Love,
Your birthmom

I can't tell you how these letters settled my mind and heart. They helped to confirm that I was doing the right thing for my baby. X & L's openness, their love for me, their lack of fear and paranoia freed me up to be glad my baby was going to them. Often I have seen adoptive parents who are scared of their children's birthmothers, and I've heard horror stories of birthmothers who have come back after months or years, wanting "their" babies back. They remind me of the story of Solomon, when faced with the two women who were fighting over the same child. Solomon said, "ok, saw the child in two and give half to each woman." One woman said, "great, do it." The other said, "No! Give the child to her, only don't hurt him!" Solomon gave the baby to the second woman. Her love for the child, regardless of her own pain, proved that she was his mother. She was willing to suffer pain and loss to ensure the safety of her child. X & L were willing to go out on another limb and trust me. They wanted to get to know me, and risk loving me, and "our" baby, even if I turned out to be like the mother in Solomon's story that wanted to cut the child in two. If I gave him to them and then later wanted him back, I may as well ask that he be cut in two, such would be the ripping of his heart, not to mention theirs. Their trust and love for me painted a thousand words.

Xylophone & Lollipop, if you're reading this, I love you. You guys are the best.

winter one

When my bed has been floating
On the flood of all my tears
Seems as though my joy has disappeared
Still I will not put my hope
In what I feel or see
I will cling to You
And trust You're holding me
But I know that Your love is unfailing
Oh, I know your grace is so amazing
Oh, I know even though my faith be
shaken
Oh, I still know that I'll never be forsaken
Cause You're always faithful
I know

Lincoln Brewster & Darrell Evans

Journal entry
January 13, 1990

My baby was due today. My friend and lamaze partner, Mary, said, "Just think. Within the next two weeks, something very major will happen in your life." It's hard to believe. People ask timidly, "Are you scared?" Yeah, I am. Only of the unknown. At this point, I'm more apprehensive about delivery than I am about saying goodbye. Something warns me that it should be the other way around. I love the parents I chose. My child will have a wonderful life, and I won't ever lose him.

Journal
January 17, 1990

When you read this, you won't be a baby anymore so I can't call you "my baby." Especially when you aren't only mine. From the very beginning you were "ours." God's, mine, and your parents as you know them. I never saw you as mine alone.

We have been through so much, you and I. It amazes me to think that at this very moment you live inside of me. I have loved you from the beginning. I have regretted what I did, but I have never regretted you.

The choice to give you up was the toughest thing I have ever done. I wished, so many times, that things had been different. But they're not. I need to look at them as they are right now. Today. I do not know what lies ahead for me, so I can't make a decision based on what might be.

I can't wait to meet you. I never expect to be "mom" to you. I chose another woman to be that, and I am eternally grateful to her and her husband for being who they are. If it wasn't for them, I don't know if I could have given you up. I wasn't about to give you to just anyone. As it is, I really feel like I'm giving you to two of my best friends to raise. Through them, I hope to watch you grow.

Even though I will always see you as my child, I will never try to take the place of your parents. I know how much you must love them, and that makes me happy.

I plan to keep in contact with your parents so they'll know what's going on with me over the years. They'll be able to fill in whatever you need to know. And I'll be here, too. Here, hopefully with your stepfather and brothers and sisters. Even if we never meet, that's okay. You can know that you've always been in me. I will do my best to move on and just let you grow. I have learned much from carrying you.

You are invaluable to me. Have a wonderful life, baby.

After he was born, I went through a period of confusion. I thought about keeping him and what that would realistically mean; where would I live, what would I do, how would I pay the bills? Eventually, I went back to my decision for adoption, but it felt good to honestly look at parenting. I knew I had left no stone unturned, and it confirmed my decision to let him go.

It was a sweet and painful good-bye letter to write. It was only a few hours after finishing it that I went into labor.

And now I see that I'm more complete every day that I can't live without You.

Rik Leaf

The contractions started at ten minutes to midnight on January 17. I had just gotten off the phone with my dad, complaining that I felt sure I'd always be pregnant and I would never have this baby. As I laid down to sleep, I had to run to the bathroom. False alarm. I lay down again, and again I needed to get up and run to the bathroom. After this happened four or five times, I called Mary.

"I think it's time. I feel weird."

"Do you want me to come over?" she asked, sleepily.

"Please!"

She was there within ten minutes, and we talked for a while. Then we decided to get some more sleep, but I couldn't. Finally, at 4:20 am, I called Nancy at the Lodge. She told me to relax, breathe, and call an OB nurse. When I did, they wanted me to come in.

This was it. I think by this time, I was so ready to have him and be out of the awkward, bulky stage, that I didn't think much about it. They admitted me to a welcoming and warm birthing room. Mary promptly fell asleep in a chair.

The contractions were getting stronger, but I could still talk over them. At 7:00, I called my sister Chris. My dad came after that and stayed for the next nineteen hours. He is a teacher and he missed two days of school to be with me. My mom, my sister Kelly, my step dad Bob, my friends; all these came and stayed through the actual birth. The room was packed. The hospital had rules about this sort of thing, but I think the doctor and nurses bent them.

When I got really uncomfortable, I requested a pain killer. All that did was numb my brain so I couldn't handle the pain as well. But I concentrated through each contraction: I was determined to stay in control and not panic. I was grateful for the training Lamaze classes had given me. By mid-afternoon I requested an epidural, which is a pain killer injected into the spine.

I hadn't wanted a spinal block, but it was dragging on so long. My strength was waning. My cervix was only dilated to five centimeters and it needed to be at ten, so we called the anesthesiologist. He tapped my spine, and the rest was a breeze. Within a half an hour I was sitting up in bed, talking and even laughing with friends and family. The nurses would comment, "Does this woman know she's in labor?" Yes, but I was grateful I couldn't feel it!

This continued until midnight. The nurses took such good care of me, and I got some rest. Flowers were already pouring in and I hadn't even had him yet.

Finally, I was dilated. My doctor almost had to use forceps, but with one final boost, Samuel was born. I had been able to faintly feel the contractions over the epidural, and with the aid of the monitor we could see when I was supposed to be helping my body push him out. It's funny how you lose your modesty at times like this. The profundity of what was happening put self-consciousness far away.

All of a sudden, he was there. Samuel Carson: a big 9 pound, 2 ounce, 22-inch long boy. The wait was over. The physical pain was gone.

Just about everyone was in tears. He was whisked off to the nurses' station because he had come out with a little infection due to the long labor. Exhaustion took me. I wanted to hold him, but I hadn't slept in two days.

Within half an hour, everyone was gone. There were lots of kisses and hugs and tears, and everyone went home to bed. It was 2:00 in the morning on January 19, 1990. I fell into the deepest sleep I think I have ever had.

We stayed in the hospital for five days. The nurses were wonderful. Whenever I needed to talk, they were there. We were waited on continually. Sam and his little crib were rolled into my room, and I mothered him there for that time.

We had so many visitors. Friends brought flowers and cards. My pastor came and dedicated him. Classmates called. I had so many gifts: the room was vibrant in contrast to the barren January outside my window.

I wept a lot during that time. As soon as I would remember that our time was short, I would melt again. People tried to comfort me, but their words fell to the floor. I knew that the decision had been made, and it wouldn't be long before Beth and the foster mother would be there to take him to another home.

At last the day did come. I had spent so many hours watching him, holding him, feeding him, rocking him. I wanted to remember everything about him. How he smelled, how he moved, how he looked. He would look at me so intently: almost like he wanted to remember me, too. I dressed him that day, and I signed the papers to release him to foster care and to New Life.

As his foster mom carried him out, he cried. I cried. The pain of finding out I was pregnant did not compare with the pain of coming to love-and then release- someone I first thought I didn't want when I found I was pregnant with him. I had grown to love him so irrevocably in the last months. The fact that he was sent as a gift by my Father to help me understand that life wasn't casual and that the actions of people affect other people deeply, only added to his worth. He was so beautiful. He smelled beautiful. That something so profound and God-like could be housed in the body of a small child overwhelmed me. What a wretch I was that I even considered taking the life of this magnificent person who would grow in the love of two people who longed for him. Who was I to tamper, even consider tampering, with his days, his time on this earth? The sorrow and grief flooded in. I clung to Pam and sobbed. And yet, hidden under the grief, I knew that I was following the road meant for us...the road that was best. It was the only thing that could have held me to it. All the months of planning and praying and releasing had brought me to this, prepared me for this. I knew so intently that this was God's best for him, and for me. I knew it. Somehow that deep knowledge held me that day. How could I have released him without that understanding?

Looking back, I can't imagine it was Pam that held me. It must have been Jesus.

Never has the weight of one been so
heavy and never has the love of a
mother been so strong.
This mother shall lift this child into
another life,
and she shall cry heavy tears.

in a letter from my friend, Dan Sundseth

Now began the three-week wait until our court date when I would terminate my rights to my son. It was a difficult three weeks because I needed to look at all my options again, and I felt like we were in limbo. He was in foster care, and I wanted him with his parents. Today, he would have been. They would have been at his birth and he would have left the hospital with them. I still would have grieved, but knowing he was with Xylophone and Lollipop would have, I think, made things easier.

Journal entry
January 23, 1990

I don't think anyone can truly understand how it feels to be sitting here without my son. I'm empty physically, emotionally. I've never hurt like this in my life.

Every time I used to eat, he'd eat, too. Every time I'd sneeze, he'd jump. I'd rub his back when he'd press up against me, I'd guide his little foot back when he'd kick too hard in one spot. I'll never forget his little face.

Jesus promises that all things will work together for those who love God. He promises to give me grace for whatever comes my way. I still have the option to keep him; sometimes I feel like I'm walking around in hopeless darkness without him. I can't imagine life without him and I can't imagine life with him. With me, he would know love, but also daycare and sometimes a busy, frustrated mother. With his adoptive parents, he would know a mom who could be with him all day. He would know a full-time, loving father and lack of want. And he would also know how much I loved him, me and my family. He would know that he has another name and another family waiting to welcome him back someday.

I miss my baby and the way he looks at me with those big, inquisitive green brown eyes. I kept telling him, "It's okay. Mommy's right here. I'm not going anywhere." He seemed to smile at that.

Love is waiting patiently to see the unfolding of God's plan. Love is trusting that God will guide me. Love is maintaining the hope that God will show me the desires of my heart. Love never fails. Love never ends.

Samuel, I lift my eyes to the hills: where does my help come from? My help comes from the Lord, the Maker of Heaven and Earth. I miss your darling smile. Our bond is so strong: I know that God will keep my love for you in your heart. He will not lead me where His grace cannot hold me. You will be fine. You will know love, joy, and contentment. He will not let your foot slip; He who watches over you will not slumber. I can offer you all that I have, but I wanted you to have more. You will have all your parents can give you; and, in time, you can have me, too.

The Lord is the shade at your right hand. The sun will not harm you by day nor the moon by night. The Lord will keep you from all harm. It was so difficult to put you into His arms instead of mine. (Psalm 121)

The days went by sorrowfully, slowly, painfully. My journals ranged from quoting Scripture to swearing in frustration. I was still living with my parents, waiting the three weeks for the court date, reviewing my options. I needed to lay it all out on the table again and again: what would it mean to parent? What were the pros and cons of adoption? I always came back to the same conclusion: adoption. Sam was in foster care for those three weeks in a town forty-five minutes away. I could visit him anytime I liked. I could call Beth and say "I want him" and they would have him to me within twenty-four hours.

I visited him three times in that three-week period. Each time I waited a little longer between visits. We would meet with friends, shop, do whatever you do in a day. Mothering him for those short times was wonderful: I would feed him, rock him, bathe him. He was beautiful. I am thankful I had that time with him.

Journal
January 24, 1990

One week ago I went into labor. I miss Sam so much it's all I can do to keep functioning.

God knows what's best. I can't give up my son! But I want the best for him! I've prayed that if God wants me to continue with this, He'll have to give me the will and the grace to do it. Hurt isn't a strong enough word to say how I'm feeling.

Anguish.

Agony.

Torment.

These come closer.

This really sucks.

January 26, 1990
Dear Lollipop

I'm not trying to exclude Xylophone, but I need to write this mother to mother. I want you to know how I feel. I want Sam to someday know what I went through... I want him to understand how I love him. I don't know what to do. I have never in my life experienced such grief.

Today is his one week birthday. I have never loved anyone like this. Everything that was so important to me before doesn't mean a thing now. All I want to do is be his mother. It's hard for me to believe that anyone else could want or love him more than me.

I made him pajamas and he wore them in the hospital, but now I sleep with them. His pictures are everywhere. I take pills to dry up my milk and my abdomen is all stretched out and flabby with stretch marks. I'm still bleeding and healing, and he is not here. My family is acting like nothing has happened and I'm in a nightmare.

I have prayed constantly, telling God that I want His best, but if that means giving up Sam, He'll have to give me the will because I can't do it. I fell like my instincts are being ripped out of me.

I need your prayers. I want to do the right thing. I can't imagine life without him, and I can't imagine life with him. He seems to need me. When I hold him he's so content and peaceful. He turns my direction when he hears my voice. He sleeps on my heartbeat and always needs to hold my fingers or examine my face. He knows me. I want him to be safe and loved and happy. I want to give him everything. But I don't want to put him in daycare. This isn't fair.

If Sam goes to you, I'll feel like he's gone to two of my best friends. But I wanted you to understand me, so you could love him more than you do now. So you could tell him how much I love him.

Your birth mom

That was a tough letter to write. After Xylophone and Lollipop had been turned down three times, I hardly wanted to turn them down again. But I needed to write that out and I needed to know what it would feel like to say, "I'm keeping him." It didn't feel right. Beth wisely waited until the court date was over and Sam was literally in their hands before she gave this letter to them. I was grateful.

winter four

I hear you have a soft spot
For fools and little children
And I'm glad; cause I've been both of those
I shook my fist up toward the sky
And at most of those who love me
A frightened, angry child in
grown up clothes
But a Father's eye can always
see right through
And a father's heart can tell
when tears are true
Now I'm standing on this road
Your hand has brought me to
Your faithful love will lead me farther on

Russ Taff

Journal
February 2, 1990

Deuteronomy 1:31 says, "There you will see how the Lord your God carried you, as a father carries his son..." As a father carries his son.

Your (biological) father carried you once, baby. He came to New Life last week. He walked in with a big teddy bear. I was holding you and you were screaming because your bottle wasn't ready. What a first impression! You settled down when I started to feed you, but when I handed you to him, you calmed completely. It was like you knew who he was.

I think he was overwhelmed. We sat together, the three of us, for about an hour. It felt weird. I felt like I was pretending, like you weren't ours.

We took some pictures of the three of us. I have so much for you, Sam. A whole box full of stuff: cards, letters, rose petals, your birth certificate, our wrist bands from the hospital, loads of pictures; I kept everything. I love you more than myself, Sam. It hurts to give you up. To trust that God will lead me farther on.

Your daddy that you grow with (your adoptive daddy) will carry you a lot, baby. He will give you more than a teddy bear. He will bandage your scraped knees and kiss away your tears. He, and she, your mommy, will do all this for you and for me.

As for me, I will cry for you and pray for you and miss you. But I will have the joy of knowing that I was the one who got to give birth to you after carrying you. I get to give your parents the joy of raising you. This is the one thing, besides knowing that Jesus is taking care of me, that is getting me through our court date. On the day I let you go forever, your life with them will start.

You won't miss me, you won't hurt. God will heal me, in time. Knowing I've helped to create a family and knowing I'll meet that family face to face someday is getting me through. Sweet dreams, baby. Mommy loves you.

I heard this once: "when you are angry with someone, you give them your day. When you stay angry with them, you give them your life." I'm beginning to understand that forgiveness is as much or more for myself than it is for anyone else. Forgiveness gives me freedom. If I am angry with anyone and stay angry, it destroys me, not them. There is a huge falsehood out there that says it is weak to forgive. This is a monumental lie! When I choose to forgive, I am in control. This is the truth: when we are angry, we are weak, because the person we are angry with has power over us. In other words, it is weakness to be controlled by anger. We may think we control our anger, we may think we have power over others when we are angry, but we don't. Our anger controls us. Think of someone who was really angry with you at any time in your life. Did their anger make you want to please them and love them, or did it make you want to get away from them? It is only when we forgive that we are strong, and it takes strength to forgive.

When I think of what it was that made me angry, in this case, my baby's father not giving me the attention I felt I needed, I don't get angry anymore. It doesn't control my day, because I have forgiven him and see the truth of the situation. Maybe he should have been there more for me, but looking back, I think that it was good that he wasn't. I think I would have been tempted to lean on him, and then I would have missed the blessings of leaning on God. And the truth is, I hurt him as well. I used him, I treated him with disrespect. It took two. If I were to hold bitterness against him—if every time I thought of him I felt this stab of resentment—then he would have control over my life and not even know it.

If we go further, think of this: God gave us everything. He gave us life and every good thing in our lives. He is available to redeem, or make good, the bad things in our lives. He is ready when we are. When we choose to reject that gift, when we choose to think we've done it all ourselves and not thank Him for his goodness in our lives, we reject Him. He forgave us when we walked away. He gave us his Son to live and die and rise for us. He gives us the choice, and total freedom to love or reject him. We deserve nothing, and yet He is kind. And yet, He forgives. The sun rises and sets. The rain comes. The wind cools our faces. He holds the power. He could annihilate us if he chose, but he extends mercy, patience, kindness. The good things in our lives are from him, whether we choose to see it that way or not.

I walked away from all of this, inviting consequences upon myself. God had mercy on me and left a blessing.

Shortly after Sam's father visited him, I received a card from him. The last thing he said was, "I like the name." We have seen each other a few times since then. I pray that he grows into a man that Sam can be proud of, and I pray that he allows God to love him throughout his life.

Two roads diverged in a yellow wood
And sorry I could not travel both
And be one traveler, long I stood
And looked down one as far as I could
To where it bent in the undergrowth;

Then took the other, as just as fair
And having perhaps the better claim
Because it was grassy and wanted wear;
Though as for that the passing there
Had worn them really about the same,

And both that morning equally lay
In leaves no step had trodden black
Oh, I kept the first for another day!
Yet knowing how way leads on to way,
I doubted if I should ever come back.

I shall be telling this with a sigh
Somewhere ages and ages hence:
Two roads diverged in a wood, and I
I took the one less traveled by,
And that has made all the difference.

Robert Frost

Thinking of things associated with motherhood brought tears instead of joy. I would never kiss his little face, watch him grow or play, or teach him about Jesus. My heart was broken. I remember something Elisabeth Elliot said in one of her books: "Pieces will feed a multitude, while a single loaf will satisfy only a little lad."

I re-read Xylophone and Lollipop's letters. I talked with Pam and Beth and Mary. I had lunch with my dad, wading through my options. I knew, again and again, that I had come to the right decision for the right reasons. What I knew took over what I felt. I had trained myself in truth for nine months, and it prevailed in the end.

Journal entry
February 5, 1990

"for the Lord your God is gracious and compassionate. He will not turn his face from you if you return to him."

I'm trying. I pray for God to hold me all the time. I said goodbye to my son for the last time today. It was my last foster care visit. I can't tell you how it feels. Of course he cried all the way out, and I kept wanting to run after him and hold him and kiss him again. I tried to notice every touch, every smell, every expression of his today. I don't ever want to forget.

Journal entry
February 8, 1990
Remember always: (to myself)

You are giving your son to the Lord, who will place him in love and safety. He would not have let you go on believing that adoption was the right thing if it wasn't. He would have told you. He loves Sam more than you do. He loves you more than you love Sam.

He has brought you through every panic attack so far. He will bring you farther. All the dark things you imagine are not from God. This is all for a reason : you had the joy of carrying Sam and giving birth to him. But it was God who gave him to you in the first place. Give him back. Don't hold so tight. Let him go.

Lord, help me to trust you.

Writing helped me deal with the grief. I went through so many stages: anger, denial, pity, wanting to fix it or change it, and just sadness. But in the end, because I had thought and prayed and talked so much about it, I accepted it. I didn't know it then, but I embraced the pain. It felt good to know that I had traversed every path, sought out every option. Writing my feelings down —my hurt and anger and frustration—trying to think of the exact words that described how I felt, was a healing process of its own. I can't fathom trying to keep those torrents inside, to let them stew and bubble. Getting things out into the light, writing them down, sharing them, brought enormous clarity.

I embraced the grief in other ways, too. Taking pictures, visiting him in foster care, sleeping with his little pajamas that smelled of his fresh baby smell: I took in all I could before I let him go.

One thing I would do differently if I could would be to read more on the grieving process. If I had, I would have seen that my feelings were normal, and that I would probably be grieving for quite awhile. That may have saved me from some painful experiences in the years to come.

What would I say to those women facing a time like this? I would say, stop. Take time to breathe and walk and not hurry. Go away if you need to: find a place like the North Shore. Surround yourself with people who love you and will encourage you in the faith and hold you accountable. Read. I've included a short reading list at the end of this book. Begin a journal. Get yourself into a good church, a good Bible study. Ask God to show you how much He loves you; ask Him to help you to see it, ask Him to open your eyes. We are His beloved, His glorious ones. His plan for our lives is exciting and more filled with life than we can imagine. There are those who walk with God consistently, and they're not usually the ones getting attention on the news. Find them in print, find them in flesh. Be mentored by them, meaning, read what they've written. Learn from them, hang out with them, watch how they live. Let them teach you how to walk with God.

The other day my family was at our park. I was sitting on a low footbridge above the stream where the children were swimming. It was only April, and even though our part of the country was having unseasonal 90 degree weather, the stream was still biting cold. The children were jumping from a fallen log into the icy water. As I watched them shriek and plunge, I though of surrender. The children were thoroughly yielding to their natural impulses to jump into that water. They were not thinking about the chill, they were thinking of the joy. They did not stop to ponder, as I would have, how cold this really would be, or if I really wanted to do this, or if it would be uncomfortable, etc. They just leaped with enthusiasm. And the stream rewarded them: they came out tingling and fresh and alive. The pain of the cold had only lasted for a moment, and then they were back on the log and with exuberance, jumping again and again. On the car ride home, after a long, warm afternoon of swimming, they could speak of nothing but the happiness of the stream.

Life sure has its choices
You've left those choices to me
and I'm glad, but sometimes I feel caught.
It's hard to know which bridge to cross
and which bridge I should be burning
I long to learn, I'm so slow to be taught

But a Father's eye can always see right through
and a Father's heart can tell when tears are true
Now I'm standing on this road
Your hand has brought me to
Your faithful love will lead me farther on.

–Russ Taff

His faithful love will lead you farther than you thought possible.

winter six

There is a wideness in God's mercy
I don't see in my own
It keeps the fire burning
That melts this heart of stone
Keeps me aching with the yearning
Keeps me glad to have been caught
In the reckless, raging fury
That they call the love of God

Rich Mullins

Winter six

February 12, 1990, was the day of our court hearing. Part of it is recorded in my journals.

It seems like a dream, but today I gave you a family, baby. I gave you back to God for His keeping. Your parents saw you for the first time today. I wish I could have been there! I would love to have seen their joy. I know how they must have felt, holding you for the first time. It gives me strength to think about it.

Tomorrow they will take you home. They must have shopped their hearts out today. I can imagine the excitement of setting up a nursery: teddy bears and the smell of baby wipes. They're probably getting ready for you now. I can't imagine they'll sleep tonight.

So tomorrow you'll bring life to that empty nursery. The quilts I made you and the sleeper of yours that I have slept with these three weeks will only be a few of the things gracing that room. I bet it's beautiful.

I feel both a peace and a pain. I love the word bittersweet. It describes so many things. I'm glad I don't have to make any more decisions. I will miss you so much, and I hate that. But you and I have brought life to a family, and I think that's worth it. As long as you're safe and happy and loved, I can deal with the hurt. I know it will fade in time, and I know this is God's best plan. Last night I laid a fleece before God. I asked Him to cause something to happen today that wouldn't have allowed the hearing to take place. A blizzard, a flat tire, whatever. But in fact, we got there without any problems, waded our way through the city, found parking, and everything was on schedule. We even got the judge we prayed for. Everything went as scheduled.

At the hearing, I sat with Beth and Pam. When the judged called on me, I had to stand and tell her why I was relinquishing my son. She wanted to know my reasons. I told her that he needed a mother and a father, and that right now in my life, I couldn't give him that. We prayed that we would get this judge; some other judges, we were told, didn't understand why a woman would first choose to give her baby life and then give him a family. This makes absolutely no sense to me. Wouldn't it be selfish of me to kill him and not allow anyone else to enjoy or love him, simply for my own convenience? Why *not* give him a family?

After leaving the courthouse, I felt a peace that couldn't have come from me. I had just relinquished all rights to my child forever, and I felt remarkably calm. I knew his parents would get a call saying he was theirs, and I knew I didn't have any more decisions to make. I slept hard during the two hour ride home.

Journal entry
February 14, 1990

I guess they were overwhelmed. Beth told me today that they hardly knew what to do with themselves. I'll bet they still can't believe that you're theirs, Sam. They probably think it's all a dream. Sometimes I do.

Beth also said that the first thing your mom said was, "Oh! You hugged her today, didn't you? Let me hug you, it's the closest I can be to her!" She passed the hug on to me and sent the message that they loved me. Your mom is a beautiful woman, Sam. I don't know if I could do better.

Dear Xylophone and Lollipop,

I can hardly describe to you the peace I feel in my heart, knowing Sam is with you. My mind is tired of making decisions. It's a sweet relief knowing God is in control.

Beth told me as many details as she could remember and that I could think to ask. I cried again. Thanks for the hug.

How is he? Isn't he beautiful? I just can't ask enough what you're thinking. I am so blessed to have carried him. He's such a gift. Don't you think?

Hold him for me. Kiss his face and tummy and toes and hands, and tell him he's fabulous and that I love him. I am so happy, but I still miss him!

Love,
Your birth mom

The dedication service was held at the New Life office the day after my court hearing. Everyone was there: Xylophone and Lollipop's parents, siblings, nieces and nephews; and they videotaped the whole thing. I'll see it someday.

Dear Xylophone and Lollipop,

How is it being parents? Day to day, caring for him, experiencing him, how is it? Does he smile yet? Isn't he just perfect?

I had my first job interview today. It went really well. I felt confident. I have this peace I carry with me: I think, "I have a beautiful son. I gave him all I had." And I'm so happy he's with you. Have I said that a lot? I am just so overwhelmed with this joy I feel. I was listening to some tapes on spiritual warfare and they reinforced the fact that we are in a battle constantly. The enemy knows us, wears us down, and waits for opportune times to attack. That is what happened to me. Little by little I compromised until one night, I could have ruined my life, or at least created and destroyed another. But God took over. I look back and can almost see the angels surrounding us, Sam and I, all the way through this.

I'm moving Saturday. I'll be working at the Lodge. The owners, Tim and Nancy, are like family. I'm looking forward to the peace and solitude. I know I have a road ahead yet; I know that this just isn't over and forgotten. I feel like I'm going home.

Thanks. I love you guys.

Once again, I gazed out the window overlooking the lake. The scene was different this time: snow covered the frozen earth, the birches were bare, the spruces dressed in their winter green. The shore of the lake was solid and snow and ice covered it for miles. Only the day before I had hiked in the woods and watched a pack of coyotes finishing off a deer out on the ice. This was the really quiet time on the Shore; I could almost hear the northern lights. My friend and co-worker, Kevin, could imitate a coyote, and we would hear multitudes of them answer as we stood listening in the sub-zero air.

It was hard to believe that almost a year had passed. My Sam was safe and happy with parents who loved him and loved me. Because of my choices, I had given life to a child and to a family. I was, and will be, eternally grateful to God for the strength He gave me.

I felt a deeper peace than I had ever known. Something told me it was an introduction of things to come. Psalm 18: 28-29 says,

> You, O Lord, keep my lamp burning;
> my God turns my darkness into light.
> With your help I can advance against a troop,
> with my God I can scale a wall.

How could I ever doubt His love again?

epilogue

And I believe what I believe,
is what makes me what I am
I did not make it;
no it is making me
It is the very truth of God and not
the invention of any man.

Rich Mullins

March 25, 1990

Dear, dear, dear, dear Birth Mom

Thank you, thank you, thank you, thank you. I have been thinking of you and saying over and over, "thank you" since the day our precious little Sam came home. He is a sweet, precious, wonderful little bundle of love. It seems as if I've known him all my life. We think of you so much. We want you to know how much we love you and the precious life that you've given us. We are having the time of our lives!

Dear, dear birth mom, you have added another dimension to our lives of what our great God has done for us. As we have shared with friends some of what we know of you, we want you to know what a picture of God you are to all of us. God sent us his only son. What a sacrifice. You asked in your first letter what it felt like, the joy that you would be giving us. It is almost unbelievable to us. We think of you and thank God for you continually.

Every time I pick up our precious boy, I think he's gained

a pound. He's growing like a weed. He loves his bottle! When he's hungry, his little mouth searches everywhere until he finds it. He's so healthy. Anytime possible, he loves his nuk.

As you know, he loves to be held, and we love it! Sometimes at night it takes him awhile to get to sleep; I think he loves life! We often have to "nuk him" for quite a while until he settles down.

The night we visited Sam at foster care was quite an experience: seeing a new son and yet leaving him until the next day, and then we came home and read the letters that Beth had given us. We wept so deeply as we saw your pain and desire to do the Lord's will. I commented that it was strange to think of one situation resulting in such contrasting emotions: your pain, loss and grief, and our happiness. Yet we wept with sadness for you to think of such a sacrifice. Sam WILL KNOW of the deep love his mother had and has for him, and that he was not an unwanted child. In this day and age, we thank God that you had the courage to make a life giving decision and pray that God will be your comfort and peace in the days ahead.

You are so precious to us! It's been exciting to tell so many friends of the process of our getting little Sam and see it be a ministry to them. Friends have told us how beautiful it is. My mom is in a weekly women's bible study. I ran into a few of them the other day and they said "We want to come and see your baby" and I said, "great, come for lunch." Eleven came! They went together and bought Sam a swing! As we ate lunch, they were asking about the adoption process, and as I told them about our birth mom and your total love for Sam, tears were running down every face, including mine.

Dear birth mom, bless you. We thank God for you daily. We love Sam more than tongue can tell. We are praying daily that we will be the parents God wants us to be, and that Sam will blossom into the person the Lord has made him to be. He is a sweet, gorgeous boy.

Thank you, again and again.

Love, X & L

I want you to know, reader, that giving Sam life and a family, and all the pain and loss that went with it, didn't make me immune to sin. We all struggle with different sin; something you struggle with may not even be a temptation to me, and vice versa. I thought I would never, ever play around with pre-marital sex again once I went through this painful trial that you have read about. Unfortunately, that was not the case. The shortened version of my continued story could fill a book all on its own, but I haven't the heart to tell it at length. The first time I had a crisis pregnancy, I was a hero. I made good decisions and I walked closely with my Lord. I was asked to speak to high school groups, youth groups, and crisis pregnancy center banquets. The journals you have read were taking on book form. I was strong, and I believe some sort of pride crept into my mind: pride that I would never succumb to this again. Somehow, I felt I was above this sin, and it was a very quiet, unspoken thought. When my doctor asked me what kind of birth control I was using and what I would like him to prescribe, I was offended. In my mind, I was never going to even think about sex again until I was married. Some friends tried to give me advice in this area, and I dismissed them.

After the court hearing, I had finished school, so I moved back to the North Shore and went to work. It was a wonderful time for me. The owner of a flower shop gave me a job and befriended me. Tim and Nancy at the Lodge loved and supported me. My roommate and I had many long walks. There were a great number of young singles there at the time, and we all hung out together: exploring the North Woods, making and sharing meals, going to church and Bible studies together, growing together. I was seeking God like I had been during my pregnancy, and He was healing me. The woods, the lake, the fresh air were all therapeutic. I remember these times as some of the best in my life.

One of the young men in our group of singles is my husband today. The beginning of our courtship was wonderful. We were both seeking God on what He would have for us and we spent many hours talking and hanging out together. All felt right then. We pursued not only our relationship and what it might hold in the future, but together we pursued the Great Romance. I have so many memories of seeing the love of God with Phil, on the North Shore. We watched our Father work things out for us, bringing us together; especially when neither of us was what the other imagined in a spouse. Our friendship grew deeper. Fairly early on, Nancy pulled me aside and kindly warned me. She said that Phil and I both had a history of promiscuity and that if God was leading us to get married, we should consider marrying right away and not prolonging our engagement. She further advised me to stay in fellowship with other Christians during our courtship, to set some boundaries for ourselves, to not be alone in compromising situations. I thanked her, but once again, to my detriment, I ignored her advice, thinking that I had this covered.

I asked at the end of the last chapter, "how could I ever doubt His love again?" I read the Old Testament and wonder how the Israelites could have continually followed after the Baal's after seeing the parting of the Red Sea, or water coming out of a rock, or their enemies routed by a heavenly army. I have wondered. But now I understand: they forgot. I forget sometimes too. I forget the depth of my sin and the huge amount of patience, grace and love that God extends to me. Once Phil and I were engaged, it was like I said to God, "Great! Thanks, I'll take it from here." We ignored the warning signs and forged ahead, to our own detriment.

I am beginning to see that when I turned from my sin and ran to God during my pregnancy with Sam, I was cleansed of that sin, for that time. But I wasn't healed of the lie that caused me to run to men to meet my needs. I was unable to resist the temptation of pre-marital sex again because I wasn't healed of the lie that said I was worthless. It didn't matter if I waited or not. I saw the love and grace of God, but I was still living according to the lies that I was ugly and unloveable, and couldn't do anything right even if I tried really hard. So after a time, I was worn down again. I got so focused on meeting my own needs and feeling the despair of loneliness that I forgot the truth. I thought I could do it myself. I forgot that I needed God.

Phil and I married in October, 1991, when I was seven months pregnant with our first child, Grace. She is called this because for a time, we were un-engaged and I was facing the nightmare again. The second time, the despair is deeper. I knew. I should have known better. I had absolutely no one to blame but myself. This time I wasn't a hero: I was just incredibly broken. A friend of mine calls it "bleeding all over the carpet." That's what I was.

Sin always has consequences: this is the plain truth. Sometimes I wonder what life would have been like had we been wise in our relationship, and had waited for sex until we were married. How I wish we had taken Nancy's advice and gotten accountability, set up boundaries, and married sooner rather than later. How I wish I had known of God's healing then, how He can re-interpret our memories with Truth as the center and focal point and heal us of the pain and the lies so we can live in freedom. Yet, God transforms our mistakes, and I thank Him that once again, he blessed us with a child instead of something more painful, but I believe we caused ourselves a lot of agony that we could've avoided. We sin and are the cause of our own pain, and God intervenes: he heals us, loves us, woos us to Him, and takes us in.

But that was not the end. I am married to my dear Phil, who is my best friend this side of heaven. I cannot tell you how much God has used this man to heal me and love me: it is like He gave me Himself in a person. I have never known someone so selfless as my husband. We had a lot of pain to work through during our first few years of marriage, but none of that compares to God's faithfulness! Phil has grown into a man of God that I could never have imagined marrying. He works hard and then comes home and loves everyone who walks through our door. He went to school and got a degree in Church Ministry and he is now the youth and young adult pastor of our church. He sweeps our children up and plays with them and talks with them and memorizes scripture with them and reads to them: He sees them. They are beautiful and talented and a joy to be with and he tells them so. Three years ago, God gave me the gift of playing piano, and now I lead worship at our church. God sent another family here to be our associate pastor and music pastor, and I have learned so much from him and his wife. The pastor we had when we moved here was just the man we needed to help us root our faith. The pastor we have now is just the man we needed to help us stretch and grow our faith. Financially, God has always come through. We have been pressed, but never abandoned. We have three healthy, beautiful, sweet little girls, beginning with our Gracie whom God gave us when we were rejecting Him again. She is such a gift, and we are so thankful for her. Our middle child, Ilsa, is funny and joyful almost always; she makes us laugh. Our youngest, Maddie, is our princess. I love being a mother, and I home school all three girls, which I also love. Blessings abound and abound, reader. I am living proof that there is life after crisis. There is life after two crises. And now, God is teaching me more and more. That His love is deeper than I ever thought possible. That no matter what relationship I had with my dad, no matter how I felt he saw me or other men saw me, God likes me and He made me because He wanted to. God sees me as pure and beautiful and worthy to listen to. Mike Bickle said in a sermon once, "He is mostly glad when He looks at you."

Of our three daughters, our youngest is the princess, as I have mentioned. She always wears dresses if she can, (I have to bribe her to wear shorts or jeans) and often has crowns on her head and "kanka" shoes. ("Kanka" is her own term for anything beautiful or "swanky": dresses, swimsuits, shoes, pajamas...if you have them all, you're a "kanka" girl.) We would often get teased in a kindly way because of her "girliness" when one day it occurred to me that she was not the one who should be chuckled at. She knows who she is. We are the ones who don't: we are all children of the King. She *is* a princess. All of us are. Young woman reading this, you are a princess. You are a child of the King of Kings and Lord of Lords, the Great I Am, the Creator of the Universe Which Cannot Contain Him. He is pursuing you. "For I know the plans I have for you, declares the Lord, plans to prosper you and not to harm you, plans to give you a hope and a future." (Jer 29:11)

It is now twelve years after having Sam, and there have been years that I have forgotten his birthday. At first I felt guilty about it, but then I realized that I was so content and healed of the whole situation that it actually rested quietly in my mind. I have not forgotten him, I just don't obsess about him. He is happy, and so am I. I look forward to meeting him; I can't imagine the joy of that day. In the end, he will have two families. Yet, we are all one in the family of God.

Open up the skies of mercy
And rain down the cleansing flood
Healing waters rise around us
Hear our cries, Lord, let 'em rise
It's Your kindness, Lord, that leads us to repentance
Your favor, Lord, is our desire.
It's Your beauty, Lord, that makes us stand in silence
And Your love, Your love
Is better than life.

–Chris Tomlin, Louie Giglio, and Jesse Reeves. Copyright 2000 worshiptogether.com songs/Sixteps Publishing

Epilogue

from the place where morning gathers
you can look sometimes forever 'til you see
what time may never know
what time may never know
how the Lord takes by its
corners this old world
and shakes us forward and shakes us free
to run wild with the hope
run wild with the hope
the hope that this thirst will not last long
that it will soon drown
in the song not sung in vain
I feel the thunder in the sky
I see the sky about to rain
and I hear the prairies
calling out your name

Rich Mullins

bibliography

Baldwin, J.F. *The Deadliest Monster*. Eagle Creek, OR: Coffee House Publishers, 1998.

Curtis, Brent and Eldredge, John. *The Sacred Romance.* Nashville: Thomas Nelson Publishers, 1997.

Elliot, Elisabeth. *Passion and Purity.* Old Tappan, NJ: Fleming H. Revell Company, 1984.

Evans, Darrell and Brewster, Lincoln, "I Know," from the CD *Freedom.* Copyright 1998 Integrity's Hosanna Music.

Frost, Robert. *Robert Frost's Poems.* New York: Washington Square Press, 1971.

Leaf, Rik. "Every Day," from the CD *Mystery.* Copyright 2001 Vineyard Songs Canada.

Meyer, Joyce. *Battlefield of the Mind.* Tulsa: Harrison House, 1995.

Milne, A.A. *Winnie the Pooh.* E.P. Dutton & Company, 1929.

Mullins, Rich. "Creed." From the CD *A Liturgy, A Legacy, and a Ragamuffin Band.* Copyright 1993 Edward Grant, Inc. (ASCAP) Kid Brothers of St. Frank Publishing (ASCAP)

"The Love of God." Copyright 1989 Edward Grant (ASCAP)
"We Are Not As Strong As We Think We Are", from the CD *Songs.*Copyright 1996 BMG Song, Inc.
"Elijah." From the CD *Songs.* Copyright 1996 BMG Songs, Inc.

Paris, Twila. "Cry for the Desert." Copyright 1990 Ariose Music/ Mountain Spring Music. From the CD, *Cry for the Desert.*

Ruis, David. "Take Me In." Copyright 1998 Howling Prairie Music. From the CD *Fragrant Oil.*

Sayers, Dorothy. *Creed or Chaos? The Whimsical Christian.* New York: Macmillan, 1987.

Taff, Russ & Tori, and Hollihan, James. "Farther On." Copyright 1989 Tori Taff Music/ James Hollihan Music. From the CD, *The Way Home.*

reading list

A Small List of Some of Our Favorite Books (To Get You Started)

*All books available from Christian Book Distributors (www.christianbook.com) unless otherwise noted. Music and movies are generally available through CBD or Amazon. If cost is an issue, try your local Public Library. You can generally inter-library loan almost any book or movie in print, free of charge, and simply borrow it from the library. I have used this service countless times.

On Living the Christian Worldview:

- *The Sacred Romance: Drawing Closer to the Heart of God,*
- *The Sacred Romance Workbook and Journal.*
- *Journey of Desire.*
- *Wild At Heart.*

by Brent Curtis & John Eldredge. (Thomas Nelson, 1997)

- *The Deadliest Monster,*

by J.F. Baldwin. (Fishermen Press, 1998)
Available through World View Academy:
1-830-620-5203 or visit www.worldview.org.

- *The Pursuit of God,*

by A.W. Tozer, 1982, 1993 Christian Publications, Inc.

- *Loving God*
- *The Body*
- *How Now Shall We Live?*

by Charles Colson. (Harper Collins, 1987) These are the books that first got us thinking about what it meant to live a Biblical worldview.

- *A Severe Mercy,*

by Sheldon Vanauken. (Harper & Row, 1977)
A beautiful love story.

- *Fresh Wind, Fresh Fire*
- *Fresh Power.*

by Jim Cymbala. (Zondervan, 1997) Wonderful books that speak of living by faith. Written by the pastor of the Brooklyn Tabernacle.

- *Always Daddy's Girl: Understanding Your Father's Impact on Who You Are,*

by H. Norman Wright. (Regal Books, 1989)

- *The Hiding Place,*

by Corrie TenBoom. (Fleming H. Revell Company, 1971). Corrie Ten Boom was a simple watch maker in Holland when the Nazis invaded. This is her story of her family's choice to hide fugitive Jews and their subsequent time in a Nazi prison camp.

- *Celebration of Discipline,*

by Richard Foster. (Harper & Row, 1978) A very practical and inspiring look at living the Christian life.

• *Passion & Purity,*
by Elisabeth Elliot. (Fleming H. Revell, 1984)

• *Battlefield of the Mind: Winning the Battle in Your Mind,*
by Joyce Meyer. (Harrison House, 1995)
• *Battlefield of the Mind Study Guide.*

• *Cry, the Beloved Country,*
by Alan Paton. (Charles Scribner's Sons, 1948)
A beautiful, haunting book that reads like a poem in prose.

• *Cancer Ward,*
by Alexander Solzhenitsyn.
(Farrar, Straus & Giroux, Inc. 1969) This one is for those who particularly love to dig into intense novels!

• *A Long Obedience in the Same Direction: Discipleship in an Instant Society,* by Eugene Peterson. (Inter Varsity, 1980)
• *A Long Obedience Journal.*

• *The Greatest Among You,* by Randy Sims.
(Worldview Press 2000) Available through the Worldview Academy website, which reads: "A must read for those who want to represent Christ well in a difficult world."

Devotionals/ Bible Studies:

• *My Utmost for His Highest: Updated Edition in Today's Language,* by Oswald Chambers.
(Thomas Nelson Publishers, 1935)

- *God, Are You There? Do You Care? Do You Know About Me?*
- *Lord, I Want to Know You.*
- *Lord, Heal My Hurts.*

by Kay Arthur. (Harvest House, 1994)

- *Becoming A Woman of Freedom*
- *Becoming A Woman of Purpose*
- *Becoming A Woman of Prayer*
- *Becoming A Woman of Excellence*

by Cynthia Heald. (NavPress, 1992)
These are excellent "beginner Bible studies."

Novels for Encouraging Reading:

- *All Creatures Great and Small,*
- *All Things Bright and Beautiful*
- *All Things Wise and Wonderful*
- *The Lord God Made Them All*
- *All Living Things*

by James Herriot. (St. Martins Press, 1966)
Phil and I call these our "comfort books" as they are hilarious and bring us to a simpler time.

- *Watership Down,* by Richard Adams.

(Macmillan, 1972) We read this one aloud as a family.

- *Anne of Green Gables,* (series)

by Lucy Maud Montgomery. (Grosset & Dunlap)

- *The Chronicles of Narnia:*

by C.S. Lewis (Harper Collins, 1955)
There are seven unforgettable books in this series

- *The Hobbit,*
- *The Fellowship of the Ring.*
- *The Two Towers.*
- *The Return of the King.*

by J.R.R. Tolkien. (Houghton Mifflin Company, 1937)
These are possibly my favorite books of all time; I could read them over and over and over. There are so many insights in them that parallel our own lives, and they bring great motivation to walk our roads with courage.
They have been called the greatest books of the century.

- *Letters to My Children,*
- *The Healing Power of Stories.*

by Daniel Taylor. (Inter Varsity, 1989)

- *Redeeming Love*
- *The Mark of the Lion series (three book series)*

by Francine Rivers. (Multnomah, 2001)

- *Christy,*

by Catherine Marshall (McGraw-Hill Book Company, 1967)

- *The Zion Chronicles,*
- *The Zion Covenant.*

by Bodie Thoene. (Bethany, 1988)

Books on the Adoption Experience:

- *The Open Adoption Experience,*

by Lois Ruskai Melina and Sharon Kaplan Roszia.
(Harper Perennial, 1993)

- *The Spirit of Open Adoption,*
by James L. Gritter.
(Child Welfare League of America, 1997)

- *Saying Goodbye to Baby:*
The Birthparent's Guide to Loss and Grief in Adoption,
by Patricia Roles. (CWLA, 1989)

- *Life Givers:*
Framing the Birthparent Experience in Open Adoption,
by James L. Gritter. (CWLA, 1989)
- *Adoption Without Fear,* by James L. Gritter. (Corona, 1989)

Guides for further reading:
When you're not sure what to read, start here.

- *Great Books of the Christian Tradition,*
by Terry W. Glaspey. (Harvest House, 1996)

- *Honey for a Woman's Heart,*
by Gladys Hunt. (Zondervan, 2002)

- *Books Children Love,*
by Elizabeth Wilson. (Crossway, 1987)

If you are experiencing a crisis pregnancy and don't know where to turn for help, you can call Focus on the Family. They can connect you with a crisis pregnancy center in your area. Their number is 719.531.3460, or 1.800.A.FAMILY.

There is also a website that can connect you with a center in your area, at www.pregnancycenters.org.